Eating out
en français

A BLOOMSBURY REFERENCE BOOK

First published in Great Britain 2004

Bloomsbury Publishing Plc
38 Soho Square
London W1D 3HB

British Library Cataloguing-in-Publication Data

A catalogue record for this book is available from the British Library

ISBN 0 7475 6975 4

Text processing and computer typesetting by Bloomsbury
Printed and bound in Italy by Legoprint

Text Production and Proofreading
Daisy Jackson, Katy McAdam

All papers used by Bloomsbury Publishing are natural, recyclable
products made from wood grown in well-managed forests.
The manufacturing processes conform to the
environmental regulations of the country of origin.

Eating out en français

General Editor
Simon Collin

French Editor
Françoise Laurendeau

BLOOMSBURY

Contents

Preface

If you have ever ordered from a menu written in French without being completely sure what you were asking for, then you need this pocket dictionary!

We have compiled this book to provide an essential pocket companion for any traveller who likes to know what they are ordering and eating. And unlike many other dictionaries, the text is fully bilingual – to and from English, so that you can easily translate a menu or ask for a favourite dish or a particular ingredient. We have included nearly 2,000 dishes and ingredients, with special chapters on wine and French cheeses (an essential part of any French meal).

This pocket book is structured in four main sections:

- English-French menu dictionary
- French-English menu dictionary
- French wines and wine terms
- French cheeses

The dictionary includes several pages of useful phrases. These have been selected to help you to find a restaurant, ask for the table that you want, order your meal, pay the bill – and, if necessary, complain.

We have also included helpful phrases for vegetarians, who traditionally have a difficult time eating out in France (where bacon and chicken are not always thought of as 'meat'!). Phrases to cover special diets are also included.

Finally, as you travel you will doubtless find new local dishes and local names for ingredients – in our experience, this is particularly so with local names for different types of fish. If you find interesting new terms that are not in this book, we would love to hear from you; please let us know and we will try and include the terms in future editions. Send any new terms (or comments on local variations of expressions) to: **frenchfood@bloomsbury.com**

Introduction

Types of restaurant

une auberge	*hotel-restaurant, usually in the country*
un bar	*serves alcoholic drinks*
un bistrot	*café-restaurant, serves drinks and simple meals*
une brasserie	*café-restaurant, choice of beer and simple meals*
un café	*serves alcoholic drinks and coffee, some serve ice cream*
un café-restaurant	*serves alcoholic drinks, serves meals*
une cafétéria	*self-service restaurant providing simple meals*
un restaurant	*proper dining room; quality can vary*
un restaurant d'autoroute	*motorway restaurant, often a cafeteria*
un restaurant gastronomique	*high quality food, though sometimes no choice of menu, often more expensive*
un salon de thé	*shop selling cakes with a few tables to have tea or coffee*

Closing times

As shops tend to shut abruptly for lunch, so, oddly, do some restaurants. Many smaller restaurants have a weekly closure timetable (fermeture hebdomadaire) – closing, commonly, on Sunday and Monday.

Tipping

Tipping is relatively straightforward: bills are often stamped 's.t.c.' (service, taxes, compris) and it means what it says – all service and taxes included. The only exception perhaps is to leave the small change in the saucer at a bar (if you are eating at the bar rather than at a table).

Public holidays in France (jours fériés)

New Year's Day
Easter Sunday and Monday
Labour Day, 1 May
VE Day, 8 May
Ascension Day
Whit Sunday and Monday
France's National Day (Bastille Day), 14 July
The Assumption, 15 August
All Saints' Day, 1 November
Armistice Day, 11 November
Christmas Day

Booking

If any of the national holidays above are part of your holiday, you should book well ahead for a place in a restaurant. Outside Paris, you should also book in advance for Sunday lunch, when large families settle down soon after mid-day to enjoy a long, noisy lunch. And don't imagine you can squeeze in for a second sitting: except for some Parisian or tourist-driven restaurants, there is no such thing.

Meals and eating times

07:00 – 09:00	petit déjeuner	*breakfast*
12:00 – 14:00	déjeuner	*lunch*
19:30 – 22:30	dîner	*dinner*

Restaurant rating schemes

Toques (chef's hats) (five toques = de luxe, one toque = fourth-class);
Michelin stars (three-stars = exceptional, one-star = very good)

Useful French Phrases

Menu

Menus are usually split into five sections:

potage *or* hors-d'oeuvre	*soup or starter*
entrée	*first course*
plat principal	*main course*
fromage	*cheese course*
dessert	*dessert*

Shorter menus might have just three sections:

entrée	*first course*
plat principal	*main course*
dessert	*dessert*

RESTAURANT L'AUBERGE

Vous propose son menu gastronomique à €34

Entrées

La terrine de canard aux pistaches
Le foie gras de canard confiture de figues
La soupe de poisson et sa rouille
Le saumon mariné à l'aneth

Poissons

Le filet de rouget au fenouil
La darne de saumon poêlée et mousse de brocoli
Le St Pierre poché aux poireaux et beurre blanc

Viandes

La fricassée de poulet à l'estragon
Le carré d'agneau persillé à l'ail
L'entrecôte grillée aux cèpes

Assiette de fromages

Le dessert de notre carte au choix

La salle à manger est non-fumeur

Prix nets — service compris

Chez Tante Claire

Menu Touristique €18
service compris

Salade aux noix
ou
Potage du jour

———•◆•———

Magret de canard grillé
ou
Poulet fermier

———•◆•———

Frites
ou
haricots verts

———•◆•———

Fromage
ou
dessert

1/2 l. de vin et café compris

Getting to a restaurant

Can you recommend a good restaurant?	*Quel restaurant nous recommandez-vous?*
I would like to reserve a table for this evening	*J'aimerais réserver une table pour ce soir*
Do you have a table for three/four people?	*Avez-vous une table pour trois/quatre (personnes)?*
We would like the table for 8 o'clock	*Nous aimerions réserver une table pour 20 heures*
Could we have a table ...?	*Auriez-vous une table de libre ...?*
by the window	*près de la fenêtre*
outside	*dehors/à l'extérieur*
on the terrace	*sur la terrasse*
in the non-smoking area	*dans la section non-fumeurs*
in the smoking area	*dans la section fumeurs*
What time do you open?	*A quelle heure ouvrez-vous?*
Could you order a taxi for me?	*Pourriez-vous me faire venir un taxi?*

Ordering

Waiter/waitress!	*Monsieur! / Mademoiselle!*
What do you recommend?	*Que nous proposez-vous?*
What are the specials of the day?	*Quels sont les plats du jour?*
Is this the fixed-price menu?	*C'est le menu à prix fixe?*
Can we see the à-la-carte menu?	*Vous avez aussi un menu à la carte?*
Is this fresh?	*Est-ce frais?*
Is this local?	*Est-ce une spécialité de la région?*
I would like a/an ...	*J'aimerais un/une...*
Could I/we have ... please?	*Pourriez-vous me/nous donner...*
an ashtray	*un cendrier*
the bill	*l'addition*
our coats	*nos manteaux*

a cup	*une tasse*
a fork	*une fourchette*
a glass	*un verre*
a knife	*un couteau*
the menu	*le menu*
a napkin	*une serviette*
a plate	*une assiette*
a spoon	*une cuillère*
a toothpick	*un cure-dents*
the wine list	*la carte des vins*
May I have some …?	*J'aimerais avoir …*
	Pourriez-vous m'apporter …?
bread	*du pain*
butter	*du beurre*
ice	*de la glace*
(slice of) lemon	*une tranche de citron*
milk	*du lait*
pepper	*du poivre*
salt	*du sel*
sugar	*du sucre*
water	*de l'eau*
I would like it …	*Je le/la préférerais …*
	Je l'aimerais …
baked	*cuit(e) au four*
fried	*frit(e)*
grilled	*grillé(e)*
poached	*poché(e)*
smoked	*fumé(e)*
steamed	*(cuit(e)) à la vapeur*
boiled	*cuit(e) à l'eau/à l'anglaise*
roast	*rôti(e)*
very rare	*bleu*
rare	*saignant(e)*
medium	*à point/rose*
well-done	*bien cuit(e)*

V Useful phrases for vegetarians

I am …	*Je suis …*
vegetarian	*végétarien (-ienne)*
lacto-ovo-vegetarian	*lacto-ovo-végétarien (-ienne)*
lacto-vegetarian	*lacto-végétarien (-ienne)*
vegan	*végétalien (-ienne)*

I don't eat …	*Je ne mange pas …*
I don't eat meat, pork or chicken	*Je ne mange pas de viande, de porc ou de poulet*
I don't eat fish	*Je ne mange pas de poisson*
I eat eggs, milk and cheese	*Je mange des oeufs, du lait et du fromage*
I don't eat eggs, milk or cheese	*Je ne mange pas d'oeufs, de lait ou de fromage*
I don't eat suet/lard/dripping	*Je ne mange pas de suif/de saindoux/de graisse de viande*
Do you have any vegetarian dishes?	*Avez-vous des plats végétariens?*
Is there a vegetarian restaurant near here?	*Y a-t-il un restaurant végétarien près d'ici?*
Is this cheese made with rennet?	*Ce fromage est-il fabriqué avec de la présure animale?*
Do you have a rennet-free cheese?	*Auriez-vous des fromages sans présure?*
Do you serve this dish without meat/eggs/cheese?	*Pourriez-vous préparer ce plat sans viande/oeufs/fromage?*
Does this sauce/soup contain beef/chicken/fish/meat stock?	*Est-ce que cette sauce/soupe contient du bouillon de boeuf/poulet/poisson/viande?*
Does this dish contain gelatine/aspic?	*Est-ce que ce plat contient de la gélatine/de l'aspic?*
Does this contain organic ingredients?	*C'est bien un plat biologique?*
Do you use GM foods/MSG?	*Utilisez-vous des aliments GMO/du glutamate de sodium?*

Useful phrases for people on special diets etc.

I am diabetic	*Je suis diabétique*
Does this dish contain nuts?	*Est-ce que ce plat contient des noix?*
I am allergic to …	*Je suis allérgique à …*
I have a peanut/seafood/wheat allergy	*Je suis allergique à l'arachide/aux fruits de mer/au blé*
I don't eat wheat/gluten	*Je ne mange pas de blé/de gluten*

Drinks

Can I see the wine list, please?	*Puis-je avoir la carte des vins s'il vous plaît?*
I would like a/an …	*J'aimerais avoir …*
aperitif	*un apéritif*
another	*un deuxième; encore un(e)*
I would like a glass of …	*Puis-je avoir un verre de/d'…?*
red wine	*vin rouge*
white wine	*vin blanc*
rose wine	*vin rosé*
sparkling wine	*vin mousseux*
still water	*eau plate*
sparkling water	*eau gazeuse*
tap water	*eau du robinet*
With lemon	*avec du citron*
With ice	*avec de la glace*
With water	*avec de l'eau*
Neat	*sans eau ni glace*
I would like a bottle of …	*Donnez-moi une bouteille de …*
this wine	*ce vin-ci*
house red	*de vin rouge maison*
house white	*de vin blanc maison*
Is this wine …?	*Est-ce un vin …?*
very dry	*très sec*
dry	*sec*

sweet	*doux/sucré*
local	*de la région*
This wine is …	*Le vin …*
not very good	*n'est pas très bon*
not very cold	*n'est pas très frais*
corked	*est bouchonné*
I would like a …	*J'aimerais un/une …*
fruit juice	*jus de fruits*
lemonade	*limonade*
non-alcoholic beer	*bière non alcoolisée*
non-alcoholic wine	*vin non alcoolisé*
low-alcohol beer	*bière peu alcoolisée*
low-alcohol wine	*vin peu alcoolisé*
non-alcoholic beverage	*boisson non alcoolisée*
decaffeinated coffee/tea	*thé/café décaféiné*
soft drink	*boisson non alcoolisée*

Complaints

This is not what I ordered	*Ce n'est pas ce que j'ai commandé*
I asked for …	*J'ai commandé …*
Could I change this?	*Est-ce que je peux le changer pour autre chose?*
The meat is …	*La viande …*
overdone	*est trop cuite*
underdone	*n'est pas assez cuite*
tough	*est dure*
I don't like this	*Je n'aime pas ça*
The food is cold	*Tout est froid*
This is not fresh	*Ce n'est pas frais*
What is taking so long?	*Pourquoi est-ce si long?*
This is not clean	*Ce n'est pas propre*

Paying

Could I have the bill?	*Pourrez-vous m'apportez l'addition?*
I would like to pay	*Garçon, l'addition*
Can I charge it to my room?	*Vous l'ajoutez à ma note d'hôtel?*
We would like to pay separately	*Chacun paye sa part*
There's a mistake in the bill	*Je crois qu'il y a une erreur sur la facture*
What's this amount for?	*Ce montant représente quoi?*
Is service included?	*Le service est-il compris?*
Do you accept traveller's cheques?	*Acceptez-vous les chèques de voyage?*
Can I pay by credit card?	*Vous acceptez les cartes de crédit?*

Numbers

0	*zéro*	15	*quinze*
1	*un(e)*	16	*seize*
2	*deux*	17	*dix-sept*
3	*trois*	18	*dix-huit*
4	*quatre*	19	*dix-neuf*
5	*cinq*	20	*vingt*
6	*six*	30	*trente*
7	*sept*	40	*quarante*
8	*huit*	50	*cinquante*
9	*neuf*	60	*soixante*
10	*dix*	70	*soixante-dix*
11	*onze*	80	*quatre-vingt(s)*
12	*douze*	90	*quatre-vingt-dix*
13	*treize*	100	*cent*
14	*quatorze*	200 etc.	*deux cents etc.*

French-English

abats giblets
abattis *[de volaille]* giblets
abricot apricot
absinthe absinthe
accompagnement *[garniture]* trimmings
acide sharp
addition bill, *[US]* check
agneau lamb
agrumes citrus
aiglefin haddock
   aiglefin fumé *[haddock]* smoked haddock
aïgo bouido Provençal garlic soup served over pieces of bread
aigre sour
aigre-doux (-douce) sweet and sour
aiguillat dogfish
ail garlic
aillé(e) garlicky
ailloli, aïoli garlic-flavoured mayonnaise
airelle blueberry
airelle rouge small cranberry
algue seaweed
aligot de Lozère potato, cheese and garlic purée
alimentation small shop selling general groceries
allumettes matches
   allumettes au fromage (fine) cheese straws
   pommes allumettes matchstick potatoes
alose shad

alouette lark *[bird]*
   alouette sans tête beef olive
aloyau *[faux-filet]* sirloin
amande (douce) almond
   aux amandes with almonds
   pâte d'amandes almond paste
amandine almond tart
amer (amère) bitter
américaine, sauce the cooking liquor from lobster mixed with the
   lobster coral and cream
amoricaine, à l' with brandy, white wine, onions, and tomatoes
amuse-gueule *[hors-d'oeuvre]* hors-d'oeuvre; *[US]* appetizer
ananas pineapple
anchois anchovy
   anchoïade anchovy dipping sauce
   anchois de Norvège sprat
andouille, andouillette sausage made of chitterlings, pork meat,
   onions, seasoning, etc.
aneth dill
ange de mer angel fish
anglaise, à l' plain boiled *[vegetables]*
anglaise, sauce *see* **crème à l'anglaise**
anglaise, sauce à l' thin crème à l'anglaise sauce
angélique angelica
anguille eel
   anguille fumée smoked eel
anis aniseed
anone *[pomme canelle]* custard apple
apéritif aperitif
arachide peanut
arêtes (de poisson) (fish) bones
aromatisé flavoured
arôme (d'un vin) bouquet
arrow-root arrowroot
artichaut artichoke
   fond d'artichaut artichoke heart
asperge asparagus
   pointes d'asperges asparagus tips
aspic aspic
assaisonné seasoned
assaisonnement seasoning

assiette plate
    assiette anglaise, assiette de viandes froides assorted cold meat; *[US]* cold cuts
    assiette de viandes grillées mixed grill
aubergine aubergine; *[US]* eggplant
au gratin with a topping of cheese and breadcrumbs
aumônière pouch-shaped pancake filled with fruit salad, ice cream, etc.
autruche ostrich
aveline filbert
avocat avocado
    avocat gratiné au four baked avocado gratin
    avocats gratinés au parmesan baked avocado and cheese gratin
avoine oats

Bb

baba au rhum rum baba
bacon bacon
baguette *[pain]* French bread
baguettes *[chinoises]* chopsticks
ballottine faggot
bambou bamboo
banane banana
    bananes flambées banana flambé
    banane verte *[plantain]* plantain
bar *[loup de mer]* sea bass
barbue brill
bardane burdock
barquette small tart *[shaped like a boat]*

basilic basil

basquaise, à la Basque style, with ham, red peppers, tomatoes

bâtonnets batons *[of carrots, etc.]*

baudroie *[lotte de mer]* monkfish

bavarois Bavarian cream

bavette flank (of beef)

bavette, bavoir (child's) bib

bayonnaise, à la braised in Madeira wine

béarnaise, sauce hollandaise sauce but thicker and with tarragon. Served warm with grilled meat and fish

bécasse woodcock

bécassine snipe

béchamel, sauce béchamel a basic white sauce made from butter, flour and seasoned milk

beignet *[pâte frite et sucrée]* doughnut, fritter
   beignet viennois doughnut
   beignet fourré à la confiture jam doughnut
   beignet de bananes banana fritter
   beignets de légumes vegetable fritters
   beignet de pommes apple fritter

belon type of oyster from Brittany

Bercy, sauce chopped shallots cooked in butter with white wine and fish stock added

bergamote bergamot

bette chard

betterave beetroot
   betteraves rouges à la crême creamed beetroot

beurre butter
   avec (du) beurre; au beurre with butter
   sans beurre without butter
   beurre blanc sauce of white wine, vinegar, shallots, butter
   beurre clarifié *[cuisine indienne]* ghee
   beurre d'anchois anchovy butter
   beurre de cacah(o)uètes/d'arachides peanut butter
   beurre de cacao cocoa butter
   beurre de truffes truffle butter
   beurre fondu melted butter
   beurre noir browned melted butter with vinegar and seasoning
   beurre noisette brown butter
   beurre sans sel unsalted butter

bien cuit(e) well done

bière beer
   bière (à la) pression draught beer
   bière anglaise blonde ale
   bière anglaise pression bitter (beer)
   bière blonde lager
bifteck steak; [US] beefsteak
bigarade, sauce sauce made from the remains of duck with Seville orange and lemon juice
bigorneau winkle
biologique organic
biscotte crispbread, rusk
biscuits [gâteaux secs] biscuits; [US] cookies
   biscuits à la cuillère sponge fingers
bisque de homard lobster bisque
blanc d'oeuf egg white
blanchaille whitebait
blanchir to blanch
blanc-manger blancmange
blanquette de veau veal stew in cream sauce
blé wheat
   blé concassé bulgur wheat, bulgar wheat
   blé noir [sarrasin] buckwheat
blennie butterfish
blette chard
blinis blinis
boeuf beef
   boeuf (à la) bourguignonne see **bourguignonne**
   boeuf de conserve corned beef
   boeuf en daube beef casserole
   boeuf stroganoff beef stroganoff
   rôti de boeuf [rosbif] roast beef
boisson drink
boisson (gazeuse) non alcoolisée soft drink
boîte (de conserve) tin; [US] can
   en boîte tinned; [US] canned
bol bowl
bombe bombe
bonbon sweet; [US] candy
bonne femme cooked with leeks and potatoes
bonite bonito; skipjack tuna
bordeaux rouge claret, red Bordeaux

bordelaise, à la   with red wine, bone marrow, mushrooms and
artichokes

bouchée (feuilletée)   vol au vent
  bouchée à la reine   chicken vol au vent

boucherie chevaline   butcher's selling horsemeat

boudin blanc   sausage of finely ground white meat

boudin noir   black pudding

bouillabaisse   Provençale fish stew

bouillir   to boil

bouilli(e) *[cuit(e) à l'eau, à l'anglaise]*   boiled

bouillon   broth, stock
  bouillon de boeuf   beef stock, beef broth
  bouillon de légumes   vegetable stock
  bouillon végétarien   vegetable stock

boulangerie   bakery

boule   flat round loaf with coarse crust

boule de glace   scoop of ice cream

boules de picoulat   Catalan dish of pork meatballs in a bean
casserole

boulette de pâte   dumpling

boulette de viande   meat ball

bouquet garni   bouquet garni *[mixed herbs]*

bouquet *[crevette rose]*   prawn

bourgeoise, à la   cooked in family style

bourguignonne, à la   with red wine, mushrooms, small onions and
bacon

bourrache   borage

bourride   Provençale fish dish with garlic mayonnaise

bouteille   bottle
  bouteille d'eau (minérale)   bottle of (mineral) water
  bouteille de vin   bottle of wine

braisé(e)   braised

braiser   to braise

branche   stick, stalk

brandade de morue   salt cod purée

brasserie   café-restaurant serving simple meals and beer; brewery

brebis   ewe

brème   bream

brème de mer   sea bream

brési   air-dried beef from Franche-Comté

brik   North African pasty filled with egg, tuna and vegetables

brioche brioche
Brocciu Corsican cream cheese made with sheep or goat's milk
broche, à la grilled on a skewer over a flame
brochet pike
brochette skewer
brocolis broccoli
brugnon *[nectarine]* nectarine
brûlé(e) burnt
brûler to burn
brune, sauce *see* **demi-glace**
buccin whelk
bûche de Noël Christmas log
buffet buffet

Cc

cabécou goat's or ewe's milk cheese, often served warm
cabillaud (fresh) cod
cacah(o)uète peanut
cacao cocoa, chocolate
café coffee
    café au lait coffee with milk
    café complet continental breakfast
    café crème, un crème (large) coffee with cream or milk
    café décaféiné decaffeinated coffee; decaf
    café express espresso, expresso coffee
    café filtre filter coffee
    café instantané instant coffee
    café liègoise iced coffee served with cream or whipped cream
    café noir black coffee
    café soluble instant coffee

petit crème (small) coffee with cream of milk
caféine caffeine
  sans caféine *[décaféiné]* caffeine-free, decaffeinated
cafetière coffee pot
caille quail
  oeufs de caille quails' eggs
cake fruit cake
calmar *[encornet]* squid
camomille *[infusion de, tisane de]* camomile (tea)
canapés canapés
canard duck *[domestic]*
  canard (à la) rouennaise duck stuffed with its own liver, in a red wine sauce
  canard à l'orange duck with oranges
  canard de Barbarie Barbary duck
  canard sauvage wild duck
caneton duckling
canette duckling *[female]*
canneberge cranberry
cannelle cinnamon
cannelloni cannelloni
  cannelloni aux champignons mushroom cannelloni
cantaloup cantaloup (melon)
cappuccino cappuccino coffee
câpres capers
carafe carafe
  carafe d'eau carafe of water, jug of water
caramel caramel
  caramel (au beurre) toffee
carbon(n)ade de boeuf beef braised with onions and beer
cardamome cardamom
cari curry
carotte carrot
  carottes Vichy carrots stewed in butter, sugar and seasoning
carpaccio wafer-thin slices of raw beef or tuna
carpe carp
carré rack
  carré *[d'agneau, de porc, etc.]* rack of ribs
  carré d'agneau rack of lamb
carrelet plaice
carte menu
  carte, à la each menu item is priced separately

French-English

carte des vins wine list
carthame safflower
cartilage *[croquant]* gristle
carvi caraway
casher kosher
cassate cassata
casserole casserole
cassis blackcurrant
cassoulet casserole from Languedoc, with haricot beans, pork,
  sausage or goose
  cassoulet végétarien vegetarian bean casserole
catalane, à la with tomatoes, black olives and garlic
cavaillon honeydew melon
caviar caviar
  caviar d'aubergine puréed roasted aubergines
cédrat citron
céleri celery
céleri-rave celeriac
cendrier ashtray
cèpe cep; porcini mushroom
céréales (froides) (breakfast) cereal
cerfeuil chervil
cerise cherry
  cerise confite glacé cherry
  cerise noire black cherry
cervelas saveloy
cervelle brains
  cervelle de veau calf's brains
chaise chair
chambré(e) at room temperature
champagne champagne
champignon mushroom
  champignons de Paris button mushrooms
  champignons farcis stuffed mushrooms
chandelier candlestick
chandelle candle
chanterelle chanterelle *[mushroom]*
Chantilly (with) whipped cream
chapelure breadcrumbs
chapon capon
charbon de bois charcoal

charlotte charlotte
  charlotte aux pommes apple charlotte
chasseur, sauce red wine boiled with shallots, garlic, mushrooms, tomatoes and demi-glace sauce
châtaigne sweet chestnut
  châtaigne d'eau water chestnut
chateaubriand, chateaubriant Chateaubriand *[thick piece of grilled fillet of beef]*
chaud(e) hot *[not cold]*
chaud-froid jelly, aspic *[savoury]*
  chaud-froid de poulet chicken in jelly, aspic of chicken
chaudrée chowder
(faire) chauffer to heat up
chausson turnover
  chausson aux pommes apple turnover
chef chef, cook
cherry brandy *[liqueur de cerise]* cherry brandy
cheval horsemeat
cheveux d'ange angel hair (pasta)
chèvre goat
chèvres en papillote goats cheese filo parcels
chevreuil venison *[deer]*
  chevreuil *[à la scandinave]* reindeer
chicorée frisée endive, frisée salad
chien de mer dogfish
chili con carne *[plat mexicain]* chilli con carne
  chili végétarien vegetable chilli
chinchard horse mackerel
chips (potato) crisps; *[US]* chips
chocolat chocolate, cocoa
  chocolat au lait milk chocolate
  chocolat blanc white chocolate
  chocolat glacé chocolate-covered ice lolly
  chocolat noir dark chocolate
  un chocolat *[bonbon]* a chocolate *[sweet]*
  un chocolat *[une tasse]* a cup of cocoa/hot chocolate
choix choice
  au choix, choix de choice of
  choix de légumes assorted vegetables
chou cabbage
  chou blanc white cabbage
  chou de Chine Chinese cabbage

chou rouge red cabbage
chou vert *[pommé]* green cabbage
chou vert frisé *[non pommé]* kale
chou vert frisé *[pommé]* savoy cabbage
chou à la crème cream puff
choucroute pickled cabbage
chou-fleur cauliflower
  chou-fleur sauce Mornay, au gratin cauliflower cheese
chou-navet swede
chou-rave kohlrabi
choux de Bruxelles Brussels sprouts
ciboule spring onion; *[US]* scallion
ciboulette chives
cidre (de pomme) cider
  cidre de poire perry *[pear cider]*
cigarettes russes sweet rolled crisp wafer filled with hazelnut
  cream
citron lemon
  citron pressé freshly squeezed lemon juice drunk diluted with
  water and sugar
  citron vert *[lime]* lime
citronnelle lemon grass
cive spring onion; *[US]* scallion
civet stew of rabbit, hare or other game
  civet de lièvre jugged hare
civette chives
clafoutis aux cérises cherries baked in a thick batter
claire type of oyster
clémentine clementine
climatisé(e) air-conditioned
clou de girofle clove
clovisse clam
cochon de lait suck(l)ing pig
coeur heart
coeur à la crème curd cheese dessert made in heart-shaped mould
coeur d'artichaut artichoke heart
cognac brandy
coing quince
colin *[merlu]* hake
colin *[lieu noir]* saithe
colvert mallard

compote de fruits   stewed fruit

compris(e)   included

compte   account

concombre   cucumber

condiment   condiment

confiserie   shop selling handmade chocolates, sweets and cakes

confit de canard/d'oie   duck/goose preserved in own fat

confit(e) *[fruit, etc.]*   candied

confiture   jam
   confiture de fraises   strawberry jam
   confiture d'oranges   (orange) marmalade

congelés   frozen foods

congre *[anguille de mer]*   conger eel

conserves   preserves

consommé   clear soup, consommé (soup)
   consommé froid   cold consommé
   consommé en tasse/en gelée   jellied consommé

contrefilet   sirloin steak

coq au vin   chicken cooked in red wine

coque, à la   soft-boiled *[egg]*

coques   cockles

coquetier   egg cup

coquillages   shellfish

coquille St Jacques   scallop

coriandre   coriander

cornet (de glace) *[ice cream]*   cone, cornet

cornichon   gherkin
   cornichon saumuré/au vinaigre   pickled gherkin

côte   chop
   côte de porc   pork chop

côtelette   cutlet, chop
   côtelette d'agneau   lamb chop

côtes   ribs
   côtes de boeuf   ribs of beef

cotriade   Breton fish stew with onions, potato and cream

coulibiac   fish pie stuffed with rice and hard-boiled egg

coulis   coulis *[sauce of sieved puréed fruit]*

coupe glacée   dish of ice cream; sundae

couper   to cut

courge   squash, marrow *[vegetable]*

courgette courgette; *[US]* zucchini
   courgettes farcies stuffed courgettes
court-bouillon fish stock
couscous couscous
couteau knife
couvert cutlery
crabe *[tourteau]* crab
   crabe décortiqué prepared crab
   crabe froid à l'anglaise/à la russe dressed crab
crème cream
   crème légère/épaisse single/double cream
   à la crème with cream; with cream sauce
   crème aigre sour cream
   crème (à l') anglaise thick egg custard made from egg yolks and milk
   crème au beurre butter cream *[filling for cake]*
   crème caramel crème caramel *[baked custard with caramel sauce]*
   crème Chantilly, crème fouettée whipped cream
   crème fleurette top of the milk; single cream
   crème fraîche crème fraîche *[soured double cream]*
   crème pâtissière confectioner's custard
   un crème, un café crème a (large) coffee with cream or milk
crème (de) *[velouté]* cream of
   crème d'asperges cream of asparagus soup
   crème de tomates cream of tomato soup
   crème de volaille cream of chicken soup
crémeux (-euse) creamy
créole *[savoury]* with rice, tomatoes, pepper; *[sweet]* with orange peel
crêpe pancake
   crêpes gratinées stuffed pancakes with cheese topping
cresson cress
   cresson de fontaine watercress
crevette (grise) shrimp
   crevette rose king prawn
   crevettes mayonnaise shrimp cocktail
croissant croissant
   croissant au beurre croissant made with butter
croque-madame fried cheese and ham sandwich topped with a fried egg
croquembouche pyramid of profiteroles with caramel, served at weddings
croque-monsieur fried cheese and ham sandwich

croquette de poisson fish cake
   croquettes de pommes de terre potato croquettes
crottin de chèvre small round goat's cheese
croustade bread or pastry case
croustillant crisp
croûte fried or toasted bread base
croûtons croutons
crudités raw sliced vegetables as an hors d-oeuvre
cru(e) raw, uncooked
crumble crumble
crustacés shellfish
cube: en cubes diced *[cubed]*
cuillère, cuiller spoon
   cuillère à café coffee spoon
   cuillère à dessert tablespoon
   cuillère à soupe soup spoon
   cuillère à thé teaspoon
cuisine cookery, cooking
   cuisine bourgeoise plain home cooking
   cuisine maigre low-fat cooking
   cuisine nouvelles nouvelle cuisine
   cuisine régionale regional cooking
   cuisine végétarienne vegetarian cooking
cuisses de grenouilles frog's legs
cuissot haunch
cuit(e) cooked, done
   cult(e) au four baked
   cuit(e) à grande friture deep-fried
   cuit(e) à la vapeur steamed
   pas assez cuit(e) underdone
   trop cuit(e) overdone
cumin cumin (seed)
   cumin des prés caraway (seeds)
curcuma turmeric
cure-dent(s) toothpick
curry curry

Dd

dacquoise   meringue filled with cream and soft fruit
dame blanche   chocolate sundae with Chantilly
darne de saumon   salmon steak
datte   date
daube   rich casserole of meat, vegetables, garlic, herbs, and red wine
daurade   bream
dé: en dés   diced, cubed, chopped
déca   decaf
  un déca   a decaf coffee
décaféiné   decaffeinated
  café décaféiné   decaffeinated coffee
découper   to carve
défense de fumer   no smoking
dégeler   to thaw
déglacer   to deglaze *[mix meat juices at bottom of pan with stock or wine]*
dégustation   tasting
déguster   to taste, to savour
déjeuner *[lunch]*   lunch; to have lunch
délicieux (-euse)   delicious
demi   half
demi-bouteille   half bottle
demi-glace, sauce   a mixture of equal parts of espagnole sauce and brown stock reduced, used as a basis for other sauces
désossé(e) *[en filets]*   filleted
désossé(e) *[sans os, sans arête]*   boned

désosser *[lever les filets]* to fillet; *[enlever les os, les arêtes]* to debone

dessert dessert

desservir (la table) to clear up

diable (à la) devilled
    rognons à la (sauce) diable devilled kidneys
    diable, sauce a sauce of chopped shallots, white wine, vinegar, cayenne pepper and coarsely ground white pepper. Served with fried or grilled fish or meat

dijonnaise, à la with mustard, or blackcurrants

dinde turkey
    dinde rôtie roast turkey

dîner *[midi]* lunch

dîner *[soir]* dinner, supper

dorade (aux sourcils d'or) gilthead bream

dorée *[poisson]* John Dory

dorer, faire dorer to brown

dormeur *[tourteau]* crab

dragées sugared almonds

Dubarry, à la with cauliflower

duchesse piped potato mixed with egg yolk

dur(e) hard-boiled; *[meat]* tough

duxelles, sauce white wine, mushrooms and shallots mixed with demi-glace sauce and tomato purée

Ee

eau water
  eau de seltz soda water
  eau de source spring water
  eau de vie fruit or nut brandy
  eau en bouteille bottled water
  eau gazeuse sparkling water, fizzy water
  eau glacée/très froide iced water
  eau minérale mineral water
  eau plate still (mineral) water
  sans eau ni glace neat; *[US]* straight *[whisky, etc.]*
eau de vie de prunelle sloe gin
ébréché(e) *[verre, assiette]* chipped (glass, plate)
échalote shallot
éclair éclair
  éclair au chocolat chocolate eclair
écorce (de citron, etc.) (lemon, etc.) peel
  écorce confite candied peel
  écorce râpée *[zeste]* grated peel, zest
écrevisse crayfish
édulcorant sweetener
églefin haddock
émincés de veau/volaille thinly sliced cooked veal/chicken, served in a sauce
endive chicory
enrobé de coated with
entrecôte rib steak of beef
  entrecôte à la bordelaise rib steak cooked in sauce made of Bordeaux wine, butter, herbs, shallots, bone marrow
entrée starter

entremets salé savoury
épaule [palette] shoulder
éperlan smelt
épice spice
épicé(e) spicy
épinard spinach
  épinards en purée creamed spinach
éplucher to peel
escalope escalope
  escalope de dinde turkey escalope
  escalope de veau veal escalope
escargot snail
espagnole, sauce sauce made from browned flour and butter
  mixed with tomato purée and brown stock flavoured with browned
  vegetables
espadon swordfish
Esquimau® ice lolly
estragon tarragon
esturgeon sturgeon
express espresso

Ff

faînes beech nuts
faisan pheasant
faisselle curd cheese
falafel falafel
far breton Breton speciality of prune shortcake
farce stuffing
farci(e) stuffed (with)

37

farine flour
   farine d'avoine oatmeal
   farine de châtaigne chestnut flour
   farine de maïs cornmeal, polenta
faux filet sirloin steak
fécule de maïs cornflour
fenouil fennel
fermier *[oeuf, poulet]* free range, farm *[egg, chicken]*
fermière with carrots, turnip, onion, celery
feuille de laurier bay leaf
feuilles de vigne vine leaves
feuilleté sweet or savoury puff pasty
   feuilleté au fromage puff pastry with cheese filling
fève bean
   fève des marais, grosse fève broad bean
fiadone Corsican lemon-flavoured cheesecake
ficelle French bread *[very long thin loaf]*
ficelle picarde ham rolled in pancake served with white sauce
figue fig
filet fillet; tenderloin
   filet de porc pork tenderloin
   filet de boeuf fillet of beef; *[US]* beef tenderloin
   filet de boeuf en croûte beef Wellington
   filet mignon steak cut from end of fillet
   filet de volaille breast of chicken or turkey
fines herbes mixed herbs
flageolet flageolet (beans)
flambé(e) flambé
flamiche northern French sweet or savoury pastry tart
flan baked custard
flet flounder
flétan halibut
   flétan noir black halibut, Greenland halibut
flocons flakes
   flocons d'avoine rolled oats
florentine with spinach
foie liver
   foies de poulets/de volaille chicken livers
   foie de veau calf's liver
   foie d'oie, foie gras goose liver pâté
fondant *[sweet]* fondant
   fondant au chocolat chocolate fudge (icing)

fondant *[meat, vegetables]* tender
fondue fondue
   fondue bourguignonne meat fondue
   fondue savoyarde cheese fondue
forestière with mushrooms, bacon, sauté potatoes
forêt-noire Black Forest gateau
forfait boissons drinks included
formule menu option
fougasse Provençal flat bread
four oven
   cuit(e) au four baked
   pommes au four baked apples
fourchette fork
fourré(e) (à/au/aux) filled (with), stuffed (with)
frais (fraîche) fresh
fraise strawberry
   fraise des bois, fraise sauvage wild strawberry
   glace à la fraise strawberry ice cream
framboise raspberry
frangipane rich pastry cream filling made with ground almonds
friand puffed pastry filled with meat
   friand à la saucisse sausage roll
   friand au jambon ham roll *[in puffed pastry]*
fricandeau braised veal
fricassée stew
   fricassée de boeuf stewed steak, beef stew
frisée aux noix curly endive salad with walnuts
frire to fry
frit(e) fried
frites (potato) chips; *[US]* French fries
friture de poissons mixed fried fish
froid(e) cold
fromage cheese
   fromage 'cottage' cottage cheese
   fromage à la crème cream cheese
   fromage à pâte dure hard cheese
   fromage à pâte molle soft cheese
   fromage blanc creamy low-fat cow's milk cheese
   fromage bleu blue cheese
   fromage de (lait de) brebis sheep's milk cheese
   fromage de chèvre goat's cheese
   fromage de lait entier full-fat cheese
   fromage frais soft cow's milk cheese, often with added cream

French-English

    plateau à fromage, plateau de fromages cheese board
fromage de tête brawn
froment wheat
fruit fruit
    fruits confits crystallised fruit
    fruits frais fresh fruit
    fruits de mer seafood, shellfish
fumé(e) smoked, cured

Gg

galantine galantine
galette pancake
    galette de pommes de terre potato pancake
    galette de sarrasin buckwheat pancake
galette des Rois Twelfth Night cake *[round puff pastry cake with almond paste filling]*
garbure thick vegetable soup of cabbage, beans, potatoes, leeks, ham, herbs, etc.
garçon waiter
garni with vegetables
garniture filling; garnish; serving of vegetables
gaspacho gazpacho
gâteau cake, gateau
    gâteau à la crème cream cake
    gâteau au fromage blanc cheesecake
    gâteau au gingembre ginger cake
    gâteau aux carottes carrot cake
    gâteau de Noël *[anglais]* Christmas cake
    gâteau de Pithiviers round puff or flaky pastry tart filled with almond paste
    gâteau de Savoie madeira cake

    gâteau mousseline sponge cake
    gâteau quatre-quarts pound cake
    gâteau renversé upside-down cake
    gâteau roulé swiss roll
    gâteaux secs biscuits; *[US]* cookies

gaufre de miel honeycomb

gaufres waffles

gaufrette wafer

gélatine gelatine

gelée jelly
    gelée à la menthe mint jelly
    gelée de groseilles redcurrant jelly

genièvre *[eau-de-vie]* gin
    baie de genièvre juniper berry

génoise sponge cake
    génoise au citron madeira cake

germe de blé wheatgerm

germes de luzerne alfafa sprouts
    germes de soja bean sprouts

gésiers gizzards

gibier (à plume/à poil) game

gigot d'agneau leg of lamb

gingembre ginger

gîte à la noix silverside

glaçage icing

glace ice
    avec glace with ice; *[whisky, etc.]* with ice, on the rocks
    sans eau ni glace neat; *[US]* straight *[whisky, etc.]*

glace *[crème glacée]* ice cream
    glace à la vanille vanilla ice cream

glace *[pour gâteaux]* icing

glacé(e) *[very cold]* icy cold

glacé(e) *[de sucre, etc.]* glazed

glaçon ice cube

glouteron burdock

glucides *[hydrates de carbone]* carbohydrate

glutamate monosodique/de sodium monosodium glutamate (MSG)

gluten gluten
    sans gluten gluten free

gnocchi Parmentier potato dumplings

gombo gumbo, okra, ladies finger

gougère choux pastry ring with added cheese

goujon *[poisson]* gudgeon
  goujons de poulet goujons, strips of fried fish or chicken

goulash, goulasch goulash

gousse d'ail garlic clove

gousse de vanille vanilla pod/bean

goyave guava

grain grain
  grains de genièvre juniper berries
  grains de raisin grapes

graine seed
  graines de pavot poppy seeds
  graines de sésame sesame seeds

granité sorbet; granita

gras fat *[noun]*
  qui contient peu de gras low in fat

gras (grasse) fat *[adj]*

gras-double tripe

gratin dauphinois scalloped potatoes cooked with cream

gratiné(e) browned; *[US]* au gratin

grenade pomegranate

grenadine grenadine

gribiche, sauce mashed hard-boiled egg yolks blended with oil
  and vinegar, flavoured with capers and gherkins, tarragon, chervil
  and parsley

gril grill *[noun]*

grillade grilled piece of meat
  grillade de veau grilled veal chop

grillé(e) grilled
  grillé(e) au barbecue barbecued
  grillé(e) au charbon de bois charcoal-grilled

griller to grill

grive thrush

grondin gurnard

groseille à maquereau gooseberry
  groseille rouge redcurrant

gros sel rock salt

grosse fève broad bean and sweet pepper salad

grouse grouse

guimauve marshmallow

Hh

hachis *[viande hachée]* minced meat
    hachis de boeuf minced beef; *[US]* ground beef
    hachis Parmentier shepherd's pie
haddock *[aiglefin fumé]* smoked haddock
hamburger hamburger
    hamburger végétal veggie burger
hareng herring
    hareng mariné pickled herring
    hareng saur/fumé kipper
    hareng roulé (mariné) rollmop (herring)
harenguet sprat
haricot bean
    haricots blancs haricot beans
    haricots blancs aux tomates baked beans
    haricots grimpants runner beans
    haricots noirs black beans
    haricots rouges kidney beans, red beans
    haricots verts green beans, French beans
harissa hot chilli paste served with couscous
heure du thé tea-time
hochepot Belgian thick soup of pork, beef, mutton, cabbage and
    other vegetables
hollandaise, sauce thick sauce made from egg yolks, a little
    pepper and vinegar, whisked over a gentle heat
homard lobster
hongroise, à la with paprika and fresh cream
houmous hummus
hors d'oeuvre hors d'oeuvre; *[US]* appetizer

hot dog *[saucisse de Francfort dans un petit pain]*   hot dog
huile   oil
  à l'huile   with oil
  huile d'arachide   peanut oil, groundnut oil
  huile de tournesol   sunflower oil
  huile de noix   walnut oil
  huile d'olive   olive oil
  huile d'olive vierge   virgin olive oil
  huile de pépins de raisin   grapeseed oil
huître   oyster
hydromel   mead
hyposodé(e)   low-salt

igname   yam
îles flottantes   floating islands *[dessert of poached egg whites in custard]*
incorporer   to blend; to mix
indienne, à l'   curried
infusion   herbal tea
ingrédients   ingredients

Jj

jambon ham
    jambon de Bayonne smoked cured ham
    jambon blanc (slice of boiled) ham
    jambon de Parme Parma ham
    jambon fumé (désossé) gammon
    jambon poché boiled ham
    jambon de York York ham (British-style)
jardinière garnished with spring vegetables
jarret knuckle
jaune d'oeuf egg yolk
julienne julienne *[cut into fine strips]*
jus juice *[of meat, fruit]*
    au jus served in its own juices
jus (de fruits) (fruit) juice
    jus de citron lemon juice
    jus de fruits fruit juice
    jus d'orange orange juice
    jus de pomme apple juice
    jus de tomate tomato juice

Kk

kaki date plum, kaki
kasher *[casher]* kosher
kébab *[brochette]* kebab
ketchup *[sauce tomate]* ketchup
kirsch cherry liqueur
kiwi kiwi fruit
kouign amman Breton rich puff pastry butter cake
koulibiac *see* **coulibiac**
kumquat kumquat

lactose lactose
lait milk
   au lait entier full fat, whole milk
   avec (du) lait, au lait with milk
   sans lait without milk

lait condensé condensed milk
lait de beurre *[babeurre]* buttermilk
lait de brebis ewe's milk
lait de chèvre goat's milk
lait de coco coconut milk
lait de soja soya milk
lait de vache cow's milk
lait demi-écrémé semi-skimmed milk
lait écrémé skimmed milk
lait entier full-cream milk

laitance soft roe

laitier dairy
produits laitiers dairy products

laitue *[salade]* lettuce
laitue iceberg iceberg lettuce
laitue romaine cos lettuce

langouste crawfish, spiny lobster

langoustine Dublin bay prawn

langue tongue
langue de boeuf ox tongue

lapereau young rabbit

lapin rabbit

lard de poitrine streaky bacon
lard fumé smoked bacon

lardons cubed pieces of bacon

lasagne lasagne
lasagne végétarienne/aux légumes vegetarian lasagne

lavabo toilet

lavande lavender

leberwurst liver sausage

légume vegetable
légumes à vapeur steamed vegetables
légumes bouillis boiled vegetables
légumes braisés braised vegetables
légumes verts green vegetables, greens
légumes variés assorted vegetables
petits légumes baby vegetables

légumineuses pulses

lentille lentil
lentilles de Puy Puy lentils *[green or brown]*

letchi lychee

lieu jaune pollack

lieu noir saithe, coley

lièvre hare
limande dab
limande-sole lemon sole
lime *[citron vert]* lime
limonade *[citron pressé]* lemonade
lingue ling
liqueur liqueur
lisette small mackerel
litchi lychee
loganberry loganberry
longe (de veau/porc/chevreuil) loin (of veal/pork/venison)
lotte (d'eau douce) burbot
   lotte de mer *[baudroie]* monkfish
loup bass
   loup de mer sea bass
lyonnaise with sautéed onions
lyonnaise, sauce sauce of onion, vinegar and brown stock

Mm

macaron macaroon
macaroni macaroni
macédoine de fruits fruit salad; fruit cocktail
   macédoine de légumes mixed vegetables
mâche lamb's lettuce
macis mace
macrobiotique macrobiotic
madeleine small scallop-shaped sponge cake
madère *[vin]* Madeira

madère, sauce a demi-glace sauce with added Madeira and butter, served with ox tongue

maïs *[plant]* maize; *[US]* corn
  maïs (en épis/en grains) sweetcorn
  épi de maïs, maïs en épi corn on the cob *[sweetcorn]*
  farine de maïs cornmeal
  maïs soufflé popcorn
  semoule de maïs *[polenta]* polenta

maison home-made, of the house
  pâté maison home-made pâté

maître d'hôtel, beurre butter mixed with lemon juice and chopped parsley, served with grilled meat or fish

malt malt

mandarine mandarin

mange-touts mangetout, sugar snap peas

mangouste, mangoustan mangosteen

mangue mango

maquereau mackerel
  maquereau mariné au vin blanc mackerel marinated in white wine

marc grape brandy

marcassin young boar

marchand de vin, sauce a sauce of red wine, shallots and stock

marché market

margarine margarine

mariné(e) marinated

marjolaine marjoram

marmelade (orange) marmalade

marmite thick stew or soup; pot

marquise rich frozen dessert of fruit or chocolate

marron sweet chestnut
  marrons glacés candied chestnuts
  purée de marron chestnut purée

marsala Marsala wine

massepain marzipan

matelote fish stew

mauvais(e) bad

mayonnaise mayonnaise

méchoui North African spit-roasted lamb

méchouia North African mixed vegetable salad

médaillon medallion *[round piece of meat or fish]*

mélanger   to blend; to mix
mélasse   treacle
mélisse   lemon balm
melon   melon
menthe   mint
  menthe poivrée   peppermint
  menthe verte   garden mint
menu   menu
  menu à prix fixe   set menu
  menu du jour   today's menu
  menu enfants   children's menu
  menu gastronomique   gourmet menu
  menu touristique   mid-price menu
merguez   North African spicy beef or lamb sausage
meringue   meringue
merlan   whiting
merlu *[colin]*   hake
mérou   grouper
mesclun   Provençal salad of rocket, lamb's lettuce, endive
meunière, à la   coated in flour and fried in butter
meurette   Burgundy fish stew in red wine
mi-cuit(e)   parboiled
miel   honey
  rayon de miel   honeycomb
mijoter   to simmer
milanaise   *[pasta]* with parmesan, tomato sauce; *[escalope]* breaded
millefeuille   millefeuille, cream slice made with puff pastry
minestrone   minestrone (soup)
mirabelle   (small) yellow plum
mode, à la   with ice cream
moelle   bone marrow
mollusque   mollusc
Mont Blanc   dessert of chestnut puree with whipped cream
morilles   morels *[mushrooms]*
Mornay   with white sauce and cheese
morue   cod
mouclade   mussel stew with white wine, onion, cream and egg yolks
moudre   to grind

moule mussel
  moules marinière moules marinière *[cooked with white wine, onions, parsley]*

moulin à poivre pepper mill

moulu(e) ground (pepper, etc.)

mousse (de poisson, etc.) (fish, etc.) mousse
  mousse au chocolat chocolate mousse

mousseline mousse; purée

mousseline, sauce hollandaise sauce mixed with whipped double cream

moutarde mustard
  moutarde de Meaux whole grain mustard

mouton mutton

muffin muffin

mulet gris grey mullet

mûr(e) ripe

mûre (de ronce) blackberry

mûre (du mûrier) mulberry

myrtille blueberry, billberry, whortleberry

Nn

nage, à la (fish) served in its stock

Nantua with crayfish

Nantua, sauce béchamel sauce with cream and crayfish butter

nappe tablecloth

nappé de coated with *[sauce etc.]*

nature plain (yoghurt, etc.), (tea, coffee) without milk

navarin lamb stew

navet turnip

navet swede
nèfle medlar
nem Vietnamese spring roll
niçoise, à la with olive oil, garlic, tomatoes, black olives
noisette hazlenut, cobnut
noisette *[de viande]* noisette *[small round piece of fillet or loin]*
noix nut; walnut
   noix d'acajou, noix de cajou cashew nut
   noix de coco coconut
   noix de coco séchée desiccated coconut
   noix muscade nutmeg
   noix de pécan, noix de pacane pecan nut
   noix du Brésil Brazil nut
   noix du noyer blanc d'Amérique hickory nut
   noix du noyer de Queensland macadamia nuts
noix de veau tender cut of veal
non fumeurs *[section]* non-smoking (area)
nonnette spiced bun
normande, à la with cream, Calvados or cider
normande, sauce a fish sauce with cream, egg yolks and butter
nougat blanc de Montélimar white nougat made with honey and
   roasted almonds
nougatine brittle
nouilles noodles

Oo

oeuf egg
   oeuf à la coque soft-boiled egg
   oeuf dur hard-boiled egg
   oeuf mollet soft-boiled egg

oeuf poché   poached egg
oeuf pourri   bad egg
oeuf sur le plat   fried egg
oeufs à la neige *[île flottante]*   floating islands *[dessert of poached egg whites in custard]*
oeufs et bacon, oeufs au bacon   bacon and eggs
oeufs brouillés   scrambled eggs
oeufs de cailles   quail's eggs
oeufs de poisson   hard roe

oie   goose

oignon   onion

olive   olive
olives farcies   stuffed olives
olives noires   black olives
olives vertes   green olives

omble chevalier   char *[fish]*

omelette   omelette
omelette au fromage   cheese omelette
omelette au jambon   ham omelette
omelette aux épinards   spinach omelette
omelette aux fines herbs   herb omelette
omelette aux truffes   truffle omelette
omelette baveuse   omelette which is runny on top
omelette nature   plain omelette
omelette norvégienne   baked Alaska

onglet   flank of beef

orange   orange
à l'orange   with orange

orge   barley
orge perlée   pearl barley

origan   oregano

ormeau   abalone

ortie   nettle

os   bone
os à moelle   marrow bone
(viande) avec l'os   meat on the bone

oseille   sorrel

oursin   sea urchin

ouvre-bouteille   bottle opener

Pp

paillasson de pommes de terre grated sautéed potato
paille au fromage cheese straw
pain bread
  pain à la farine de maïs corn bread
  pain au chocolat rectangular croissant-style pastry with chocolate filling
  pain aux noix walnut bread
  pain aux raisins round croissant-style pastry with raisins
  pain blanc white loaf, white bread
  pain bis brown bread
  pain complet wholemeal bread
  pain croustillant crisp bread
  pain de campagne farmhouse loaf
  pain d'épice(s) gingerbread
  pain de mie white sandwich loaf
  pain de seigle rye bread
  pain de son wholemeal bread
  pain de viande meat loaf
  pain grec *[sans levain]* pitta bread
  pain grillé *[rôtie]* toast
  pain moulé pan loaf
  pain noir de Westphalie pumpernickel bread
  pain perdu French toast
palmier large crisp biscuit of flaky pastry
palourde clam
pamplemousse grapefruit
  jus de pamplemousse grapefruit juice
panaché *[boisson]* shandy
panaché de mixed plate of
  panaché de légumes selection of vegetables, mixed vegetables

French-English

panais parsnip

pan bagnat Provençal hollowed-out roll filled with tomatoes, green peppers, olives, onions, anchovies

pané(e) breaded

papaye papaya, pawpaw

paprika paprika

parfait parfait
   parfait au café coffee parfait

Paris-Brest cake of chou pastry with praline filling

Parmentier with potatoes

parmesan Parmesan (cheese)

pastèque watermelon

pastis aniseed-flavoured aperitif mixed with water, particularly popular in the South

patate douce sweet potato; *[US]* yam

pâte pastry
   pâte à choux choux pastry
   pâte à frire batter
   pâte brisée shortcrust pastry
   pâte feuilletée puff pastry

pâte *[on cheese]* rind

pâte d'amandes almond paste

pâté pâté
   pâté de campagne coarse pork pâté
   pâté de canard duck paté
   pâté de foie gras liver pâté
   pâté de soja tofu
   pâté de gibier en croûte game pie

pâtes (alimentaires) pasta
   pâtes fraîches fresh pasta

paté en croûte meat pie

pâté végétal vegetable pie

pâtisserie French pastry; cake

patte leg
   pattes de dinde/de poulet turkey/chicken drumsticks

paupiette thin rolled stuffed piece of meat
   paupiette de boeuf beef olive
   paupiette de veau veal olive

pavé square or rectangular piece of steak, cheese, etc.

paysanne served with carrots, turnips, onions, celery, potatoes, bacon

peau skin, peel
  sans peau peeled
pêche peach
peler to peel
pelure peel
  sans pelure peeled
perche d'eau douce perch
perdreau young partridge
perdrix partridge
périgourdine, à la with truffles, liver pâté
persil parsley
  persil frisé curly parsley
  persil plat flat parsley
persillé(e) garnished with chopped parsley
pétillant(e) sparkling, fizzy
petit beurre butter biscuit
petit déjeuner breakfast
petit pain (bread) roll, bap
  petit pain au lait bun
  petit pain au seigle rye bread roll
petits fours petits fours *[small dessert or cake]*
petits pois green peas, garden peas
  petits pois gourmands, pois mange-tout mangetout, sugar snap
  peas
petit-suisse cream cheese in a pot, eaten with sugar
petits gris small dark brown snails
pets de nonne deep-fried fritters often served hot with sugar
pichet carafe
  un pichet de rouge a carafe of red wine
pickles pickles
pieds de porc pig's trotters
pieds et paquets Provençal stuffed parcels of sheep's tripe cooked
  with trotters, wine, herbs and tomatoes
pigeon pigeon
pigeonneau squab
pignon pine nut
pilaf aux champignons mushroom pilaff
pilchard *[grosse sardine]* pilchard
piment doux *[poivron]* pepper, capsicum
  piment fort, piment rouge chilli, red chilli, chilli pepper
  piment (fort) en poudre chilli powder

piment de la Jamaïque   allspice
pimprenelle   burnet
pintade   guinea fowl
piperade   peppers, onions, garlic and tomatoes with beaten eggs and
   sometines ham
piquant(e)   hot *[strong]*
pissaladière   Provençal tart with onions, olives, tomatoes,
   anchovies
pistache   pistachio (nut)
pistou   (basil) pesto
plaquemine *[kaki]*   persimmon
plat   dish
   plat du jour   dish of the day
   plat principal   main course; *[US]* entree
plateau à fromage, plateau de fromages   cheese board
pleurote   oyster mushroom
plie   plaice
poché(e)   poached
   poché dans du lait   poached in milk
pocher   to poach
pochouse   Burgundian stew of freshwater fish in white wine
poêlé(e)   pan-fried
point, à *[rose]*   medium-rare
pointes d'asperges   asparagus tips
poire   pear
   poires au vin de Bourgogne   pears poached in red wine
poireau   leek
   petits poireaux   baby leeks
pois   pea
   petits pois   green peas, garden peas
   pois cassés   split peas
   pois chiche   chickpea
   pois gourmands, pois mange-tout, mangetouts   mangetout
poisson   fish
   poisson d'eau douce   freshwater fish, river fish
   poisson de mer   sea fish
   poisson frit   fried fish
   poisson fumé   smoked fish
   poisson plat   flat fish
   poisson volant   flying fish
poisson-chat *[silure]*   catfish

poitrine breast
    poitrine d'agneau/de veau breast of lamb/veal
    poitrine de boeuf brisket of beef

poivrade, sauce a mix of vegetables cooked with wine, vinegar, pepper, and demi-glace sauce

poivre pepper *[spice]*
    moulin à poivre pepper mill
    poivre de cayenne cayenne pepper
    poivre en grains whole pepper
    poivre moulu ground pepper
    poivre noir/vert/blanc black/green/white pepper

poivrière pepper pot

poivron pepper *[vegetable]*
    poivron farci stuffed pepper
    poivron rouge *[piment doux]* red pepper
    poivron vert green pepper

polenta *[semoule de maïs]* polenta

pomme *[fruit]* apple
    pomme au four baked apple
    purée de pommes apple puree

pomme (de terre) potato
    pomme de terre au four baked potato
    pommes (de terre) dauphine croquettes of mashed potatoes mixed with choux pastry
    pommes (de terre) dauphinoises sliced potatoes baked with milk, cream, eggs and seasoning
    pommes (de terre) duchesse duchesse potatoes *[mashed and mixed with egg yolk, baked]*
    pommes de terre à l'anglaise/à l'eau boiled potatoes
    pommes de terre aux amandes amandine potatoes
    pommes de terre nouvelles new potatoes
    pommes de terre sautées fried potoatoes
    pommes allumettes matchstick potatoes
    pommes chips (potato) crisps; *[US]* potato chips
    pommes frites (potato) chips; *[US]* French fries
    pommes mousseline puréed potatoes
    pommes purée mashed potatoes; *[US]* creamed potatoes

porc pork

porcelet suckling pig

pot jug

pot au chocolat chocolate pot

pot au feu braised meat or poultry and vegetables, with the broth served separately

potage soup
   potage au cari mulligatawny (soup)
   potage aux légumes vegetable soup
   potage bonne femme leek and potato soup
   potage St Germain green pea soup

potée thick soup or stew of pork, ham, cabbage, beans and other
   vegetables

potiron *[citrouille]* pumpkin

pouding fruit or milk pudding
   pouding au riz *[cuit au four]* rice pudding
   pouding cabinet cabinet pudding
   pouding de Noël *[anglais]* Christmas pudding

poularde fattened chicken

poule boiling fowl

poulet chicken
   poulet à la Kiev chicken kiev
   poulet frit fried chicken
   poulet rôti roast chicken

poulpe octopus

pourboire tip, gratuity

pourpier purslane

poussin poussin

poutassou blue whiting

pré-cuit(e) par-boiled

présure rennet
   sans présure rennet-free

primeurs new season's fruit/vegetables

prix price
   à prix fixe set, fixed-price

profiteroles profiteroles

propre clean

provençale, à la with tomatoes, garlic, olive oil, olives

prune plum
   prune de Damas damson

pruneau (sec) prune

prunelle sloe
   eau de vie de prunelle sloe gin

purée puree
   en purée mashed (potatoes); stewed (fruit)
   purée de pois mushy peas
   purée de pois cassés pease-pudding

purée de pommes   apple puree, apple sauce
purée de pommes de terre, pommes purée   mashed potatoes; *[US]* creamed potatoes

Qq

quark *[fromage blanc]*   quark
quatre-épices   allspice
quenelles *[de brochet, de poulet ou veau]*   quenelles *[oval dumplings of pike, chicken or veal, poached]*
quetsche   dark red plum
queue de boeuf   oxtail
  soupe à la queue de boeuf   oxtail soup
queues de langoustine *[scampi]*   scampi
quiche   quiche
  quiche lorraine   quiche lorraine
  quiche au saumon fumé   smoked salmon quiche

Rr

râble (de lapin/lièvre) saddle (of rabbit/of hare)

radis radish, radishes

rafraîchi(e) chilled

rafraîchisseur *[à vin]* wine cooler

ragoût *[fricassée]* stew
   ragoût de boeuf *[potée]* hotpot
   ragoût de mouton à l'irlandaise Irish stew

raie skate

raifort horseradish

raifort, sauce a mixture of grated horseradish, vinegar and
   whipped cream. Served with roast beef and smoked fish

raisin(s) *[de table]* grape(s)
   raisins de Corinthe currants
   raisins de Smyrne sultanas
   raisins sec raisins

ramequin ramekin

rance rancid

râpé(e) grated

rascasse scorpion fish

rassis(e) stale

ratatouille ratatouille

ravigote, sauce a vinaigrette made with oil and vinegar, egg yolk,
   capers, parsley, tarragon, chervil, chives, and onion

ravioli ravioli

recette recipe

réglisse liquorice

reine-claude greengage (plum)

relever to spice up

rémoulade, sauce mayonnaise with capers, gherkins, anchovy.
  Served with fried fish

repas meal

requin shark

rhubarbe rhubarb

rhum rum

rillettes shredded potted pork or goose

rillons fried pieces of crispy pork or goose

ris de veau sweetbreads

rissole rissole

riz rice
  riz au blanc, riz à la chinoise boiled rice
  riz au lait au four baked rice, rice pudding
  riz Caroline long-grained rice
  riz complet brown rice
  riz indien basmati rice
  riz pour risotto risotto rice
  riz rond pudding rice
  riz sauvage wild rice

Robert, sauce fried onion with stock, mustard, and castor sugar
  added. Served with fried pork chop

rognon kidney
  rognons à la (sauce) diable devilled kidneys

romaine *[laitue]* romaine lettuce, cos lettuce

romarin rosemary

romsteck rump steak

roquette rocket

rosbif roast beef

rôti roast
  rôti de boeuf *[rosbif]* roast beef
  rôti de porc roast pork

rôti(e) roasted

rôtie *[pain grillé]* toast

rôtir to roast

rouget barbet red mullet

rouille mayonnaise made of chillies, garlic, and olive oil

roulade stuffed rolled (meat etc.)

roux a mixture of fat and flour cooked together, used as the base for
  sauces

russe, à la served with sour cream, hard-boiled egg and beetroot

rye *[whisky de seigle]* rye whisky

Ss

sabayon zabaglione
sablé shortbread
saccharine saccharin
safran saffron
sagou sago
saignant(e) *[viande]* rare *[meat, steak]*
saindoux lard
Saint Germain with green peas
Saint-Pierre dory, John Dory
saisir to sear
salade salad; lettuce
  salade au poulet chicken salad
  salade César Caesar salad
  salade composée mixed salad *[containing vegetables, meat or eggs, fish etc.]*
  salade de fruits fruit salad
  salade de pommes de terre potato salad
  salade de tomate tomato salad
  salade mixte lettuce and tomato salad
  salade niçoise salad of tomatoes, hard-boiled eggs, olives, anchovies, green beans, capers, potatoes, lettuce, green pepper, cucumber and/or tuna
  salade panachée mixed salad
  salade tiède warm salad
  salade verte green salad
  salade Waldorf *[pommes, céleri, noix, avec mayonnaise]* Waldorf salad
sale dirty *[plate, tablecloth, etc.]*

French-English

salé(e) salted; salty

salir to dirty

salmis game bird served in rich wine sauce made with remains of bird

salsifis salsify

sandre pike-perch

sandwich sandwich
  sandwich au fromage cheese sandwich
  sandwich au jambon ham sandwich

sanglier boar

sardine sardine

sarrasin *[blé noir]* buckwheat

sarriette savoury *[herb]*

sauce *[jus de viande]* sauce; gravy

sauce *[mayonnaise; vinaigrette]* dressing

sauce sauce
  sauce à l'aneth dill sauce
  sauce à la crème cream sauce
  sauce à la menthe (fraîche) mint sauce
  sauce au beurre butter sauce
  sauce au chocolat chocolate sauce
  sauce au pain bread sauce
  sauce aux canneberges cranberry sauce
  sauce bigarade *[bitter]* orange sauce
  sauce blanche *[béchamel]* white sauce
  sauce béarnaise béarnaise (sauce)
  sauce bordelaise bordelaise (red wine) sauce
  sauce diable devilled sauce
  sauce espagnole brown sauce
  sauce hollandaise hollandaise sauce
  sauce madère Madeira sauce
  sauce Mornay cheese sauce
  sauce soja soy sauce, soya sauce
  sauce tartare tartar(e) sauce
  sauce tomate tomato sauce

saucisse sausage
  saucisse de Toulouse fat pork sausage

saucisson French sausage (pre-cooked)
  saucisson italien salami

sauge sage

saumon salmon
  saumon fumé smoked salmon
  darne de saumon salmon steak

sauté(e) sautéed

sauter à la chinoise to stir-fry

sautoir sauté pan
  au sautoir sautéd

saxifrage saxifrage

scampi scampi

seau de glace bucket of ice

sec (sèche) dry
  très sec very dry *[wine]*

séché(e) dried

seiche cuttlefish

seigle rye

sel salt
  qui contient peu de sel low-salt (dish)
  sel gemme rock salt

selle (d'agneau) saddle

semoule semolina

serpolet wild thyme

serveur waiter

serveuse waitress

service service
  service compris service included
  service non compris service not included
  service à la discrétion du client service discretionary

serviette (de table) napkin, serviette

sésame sesame seed

silure *[poisson-chat]* catfish

sirop syrup
  sirop de maïs corn syrup
  sirop d'érable maple syrup

socca chickpea flour pancake

soja (fève de) soy bean, soya bean
  sauce soja soy sauce, soya sauce

sole Dover sole; sand sole

sommelier wine waiter

son (de blé) bran

sorbet sorbet

sorgho sorghum

Soubise, sauce béchamel sauce with onion purée, flavoured with nutmeg. Used for roast meats

soucoupe saucer

soufflé soufflé
  soufflé au fromage cheese soufflé
  soufflé aux fraises strawberry soufflé
soupe soup
  soupe à la queue de boeuf oxtail soup
  soupe à l'oignon onion soup
  soupe au pistou Provençal soup of vegetables, noodles, beans, basil
  soupe aux légumes vegetable soup
  soupe aux pois (cassés) pea soup *[with split peas]*
  soupe de poisson(s) fish soup
  soupe de poulet chicken soup
souris d'agneau knuckle-end of leg of lamb (on the bone)
spaghetti spaghetti
sprat *[harenguet]* sprat
steak steak
  steak au poivre pepper steak
  steak (et) frites steak and chips
  steak tartare raw minced fillet steak served with raw egg yolk, capers, onions
stoemp Belgian dish of mashed potato and chopped vegetables
stout *[bière brune]* stout
stroganoff de champignons mushroom stroganoff
strudel aux pommes apple strudel
succédané de lait *[en poudre]* coffee whitener
sucre sugar
  sucre de canne cane sugar
  sucre d'érable maple sugar
  sucre d'orge barley sugar
  sucre glace, sucre en poudre icing sugar
  sucre roux *[cassonade]* (soft) brown sugar
  sucre semoule caster sugar
  sucre vanillé vanilla sugar
sucré(e) sweet
suif (de boeuf) suet
supplément supplement
  supplément légumes €3 vegetables €3 extra
suprême de poulet *[blanc, filet]* chicken breast, breast of chicken
surgelé(e) frozen
syllabub *[sabayon]* syllabub

Tt

table table
taboulé tabouleh
tagliatelle tagliatelle
  tagliatelles aux champignons et à la crème creamy mushroom
  tagliatelle
tajine North African stew simmered in conical earthenware dish
tamiser to sift
tanche tench
tangerine tangerine
tapenade paste made of black olives, capers, lemon, anchovies,
  olive oil
taploca tapioca
tartare *see* **steak tartare**
tarte pie
  part de tarte slice of pie
  tarte à l'oignon onion tart
  tarte aux fruits fruit tart
  tarte aux noix de pécan pecan pie
  tarte aux pommes apple pie
  tarte Tatin upside down apple pie *[apples covered with pastry
  served upside down]*
tartelette (small) tart
  tartelette à la crème custard tart
  tartelette aux pommes apple tart
tartine slice of bread and butter
tasse cup
  tasse à café coffee cup
  tasse à thé tea cup

tasse de café   cup of coffee
tasse de chocolat   cup of cocoa/hot chocolate
tasse de thé   cup of tea
tasse et soucoupe   cup and saucer
tendre *[viande]*   tender
terrine   terrine *[chopped fish, meat or vegetable loaf]*
thé   tea
  thé (au) citron   lemon tea
  thé au lait   tea with milk
  thé de Chine   China tea
  thé glacé   iced tea
  thé japonais   Japan tea
  thé nature   tea without milk or sugar
  thé vert   green tea
théière   teapot
thon   tuna, tunny
  thon blanc   albacore (tuna)
thym   thyme
tian   Provençal gratin of fish or vegetables cooked in a shallow dish
tiède   warm, not hot or cold *[salad etc.]*
tilleul   lime
timbale   cup-shaped mould
  timbale de poisson   fisherman's pie
tire-bouchon   corkscrew
tisane   herbal tea
tofu *[pâté de soja]*   tofu
toilettes   lavatory, toilet
tomate   tomato
  tomate-cerise   cherry tomato
  tomate oblongue/italienne   plum tomato
  tomates farcis   stuffed tomatoes
  tomates séchées (au soleil)   sun-dried tomatoes
topinambour   Jerusalem artichoke
torsade   twisted plait
tourin   cream of onion soup
tournedos   fillet steak
tournesol   sunflower
  graines de tournesol   sunflower seeds
  huile de tournesol   sunflower oil
tourte   tart or flan with puff pastry
tourteau *[crabe]*   crab
tranche   slice
  tranche de jambon   slice of ham

French-English

tranche de pain   slice of bread
tranche napolitaine   Neapolitan ice cream
tranché(e)   sliced (bread, etc.)
travers de porc   spare ribs
tremper   to dip
trévise *[chicorée rouge]*   radicchio
tripes   tripe
tripes à la mode de Caen   tripe cooked with vegetables and white wine, for 7 to 8 hours
trou normand   glass of Calvados or other spirits between courses to clear the palate
truffade   Auvergne dish of potatoes, bacon, cheese and garlic, eaten with sausages
truffe   truffle
truffé   garnished with truffle
truffe au chocolat   chocolate truffle
truite   trout
truite arc-en-ciel   rainbow trout
truite de mer   sea trout
truite saumonée   salmon trout
tuile aux amandes   thin almond biscuit similar to brandy snap
turbot   turbot

Vv

vacherin   meringue filled with ice cream or cream
vaisselle *[service de porcelaine]*   china (service)
vanille   vanilla
extrait de vanille   vanilla essence
glace à la vanille   vanilla ice cream
vapeur   steamed
veau *[animal]*   calf

veau *[viande]* veal
    escalope de veau veal escalope
    foie de veau calf's liver
    noix de veau tender cut of veal

végétalien (-ienne) vegan

végétarien (-ienne) vegetarian

velouté (de) cream (of) *[soup]*
    velouté de champignons cream of mushroom soup

velouté, sauce a white sauce made from fat and flour cooked till lightly coloured, with added white stock

venaison venison

vermicelle vermicelli

verre glass
    verre à eau glass for water
    verre à vin wine glass
    verre d'eau glass of water
    verre de vin glass of wine
    verre propre clean glass

verte, sauce mayonnaise mixed with tarragon or chervil, chives and watercress

verveine lemon verbena

viande meat
    viande de cheval horse meat
    viande en cocotte pot roast
    viande froide cold meat
    viande fumé smoked meat

vichyssoise vichyssoise *[leek and cream soup]*

viennoiserie croissants, brioches, pains aux raisins, etc

vigneronne, à la served with grapes and a wine sauce

vin wine
    vin blanc white wine
    vin corsé full-bodied wine
    vin de Bordeaux Bordeaux wine
    vin de Bourgogne Burgundy wine
    vin de pays local wine of a particular grape variety and area
    vin de Porto port
    vin de table table wine
    vin doux, vin de dessert dessert wine, sweet wine
    vin léger light-bodied wine
    vin local local wine
    vin (de la) maison house wine
    vin mousseux; vin pétillant sparkling wine
    vin rosé rosé (wine)
    vin rouge red wine

French-English

French-English

vin sec dry wine
vinaigre vinegar
    vinaigre balsamique balsamic vinegar
    vinaigre de cidre cider vinegar
    vinaigre de vin (rouge/blanc) (red/white) wine vinegar
vinaigrette French dressing, vinaigrette
vivaneau red snapper
volaille fowl; chicken
vol-au-vent *[bouchée feuilletée; timbale]* vol au vent

WwZz

waterzooi Belgian dish of chicken cooked in stock, white wine and
    cream with vegetables
WC toilet, lavatory
whiskey irlandais Irish whiskey
whisky écossais whisky
xérès sherry
yaourt yoghurt
    yaourt à la grecque Greek yoghurt
    yaourt nature plain yoghurt
    yaourt aux myrtilles blueberry yoghurt
yoghourt yoghurt
zabaglione zabaglione
zeste *[écorce râpée]* zest
    zeste de citron lemon zest, grated lemon peel

English-French

Aa

abalone ormeau
absinthe absinthe
account compte
aïloli sauce ailloli, aïoli
air-conditioned climatisé(e)
albacore (tuna) thon blanc, germon
ale bière (anglaise) blonde; *see also* **beer**
alfalfa sprouts germes de luzerne
allergic allergique (à/au/aux...)
allergy allergie (à/au/aux...)
allspice piment de la Jamaïque
almond amande douce
  almond paste pâte d'amandes
  with almonds aux amandes
amandine potatoes pommes de terre aux amandes
anchovy anchois
  anchovy butter beurre d'anchois
  anchovy paste purée, pâte d'anchois
angel (food) cake angel cake *[génoise sans jaune d'oeufs]*
angel fish ange de mer
angel hair pasta cheveux d'ange
angels on horseback angels on horseback *[huîtres entourées de bacon, grillées, sur toast]*
angelica angélique
angler baudroie, lotte (de mer)
aniseed anis
aperitif apéritif

74

appetizer [US] [drink] apéritif;
   [food] amuse-gueule; hors-d'oeuvres
apple pomme [fruit]
  apple fritter beignet de pommes
  apple juice jus de pomme
  apple pie tarte aux pommes
  apple puree purée de pommes
  apple sauce purée de pommes [peu sucrée]
  apple strudel strudel aux pommes
  apple turnover chausson aux pommes
  apple tart tartelette aux pommes
apricot abricot
aroma arôme; bouquet [of wine]
arrowroot arrow-root
artichoke artichaut
ashtray cendrier
asparagus asperge
  asparagus tips pointes d'asperges
aspic aspic
assorted vegetables choix de légumes, légumes variés
aubergine aubergine
au gratin [US] gratiné(e), au gratin
avocado avocat

Bb

baby petit
  baby corn (cob) tout petit épi de maïs
  baby leeks petits poireaux
  baby vegetables petits légumes
bacon bacon, lard fumé
  bacon and eggs oeufs au bacon

bad mauvais(e)
  bad egg oeuf pourri
bake (faire) cuire au four
baked cuit(e) au four
  baked Alaska omelette norvégienne
  baked apple pomme au four
  baked beans haricots blancs aux tomates; fèves au lard
  baked custard flan
  baked potato pomme de terre au four
  baked rice riz au lait au four, pouding au riz
bakery boulangerie; *[for cakes]* patisserie
balsamic vinegar vinaigre balsamique
banana banane
  banana fritter beignet de bananes
  banana split banana split *[banane, glace à la vanille, Chantilly, amandes]*
  banana flambé banane flambée
Barbary duck canard de Barbarie
barbecue barbecue
barbecued grillé(e) au barbecue
barbel rouget barbet
barley orge
  barley sugar sucre d'orge
  barley water sirop d'orgeat *[fait avec de l'orge]*
basil basilic
  basil pesto pistou
basmati rice riz indien, riz Caroline
bass loup (de mer), bar
batons *[of carrots, etc.]* bâtonnets
batter pâte à frire
Bavarian cream bavarois
bay leaf feuille de laurier
bean haricot
  bean sprouts germes de soja
  broad beans grosses fèves; fèves des marais
  French beans, green beans, string beans haricot verts
  kidney beans haricots rouges
  runner beans haricots grimpants
  soya bean (fève de) soja
béarnaise (sauce) sauce béarnaise
béchamel (sauce) (sauce) béchamel
beech nuts faînes

beef boeuf
  beefsteak *[US]* bifteck, steak
  beef stock bouillon de boeuf
  beef Wellington filet de boeuf en croûte
  roast beef rosbif
beer bière
  draught beer bière (à la) pression
beetroot betterave
bergamot bergamote
bib *[child's]* bavette, bavoir
bilberry airelle, myrtille
bill addition
biscuits biscuits, gâteaux secs
bitter amer (amère)
bitter bière anglaise pression
black butter beurre noir
black beans haricots noirs
blackberry mûre (de ronce)
black cherry cerise noire
black coffee café noir
blackcurrant cassis *[groseille noire]*
Black Forest cake/gateau forêt-noire
black halibut flétan noir
black pepper poivre noir
black pudding boudin noir
blaeberry airelle, myrtille
blanch blanchir
blancmange blanc-manger
blend mélanger, incorporer
blinis blinis
blueberry myrtille, bleuet
blue cheese fromage bleu
blue whiting poutassou
boar sanglier; *[young]* marcassin
boil (faire) bouillir
boiled bouilli(e), cuit(e) à l'eau, à l'anglaise
  boiled egg oeuf à la coque
  boiled ham jambon poché
  boiled potatoes pommes de terre à l'anglaise/à l'eau
  boiled rice riz au blanc, riz à la chinoise
  hard-boiled egg oeuf dur

English-French

bombe bombe
bone os
   boned désossé(e) *[viande, poisson]*
   on the bone *[meat]* avec l'os; *[fish]* dont les arêtes n'ont pas été retirées
   bones (of fish) arêtes (de poisson)
bonito bonite
borage bourrache
bordelaise sauce sauce bordelaise
borlotti beans haricots italiens
bouquet garni bouquet garni
bottle bouteille
   bottle opener ouvre-bouteille
bowl bol
brains cervelle (de veau)
braise braiser
braised braisé(e)
bran son (de blé)
brandy cognac
   cherry brandy cherry brandy, liqueur de cerise
brawn fromage de tête
Brazil nut noix du Brésil
bread pain
   breadcrumbs chapelure
   bread knife petit couteau *[pour beurrer son pain]*
   bread sauce sauce au pain
breaded pané(e)
breakfast petit déjeuner
bream brème (de mer)
breast poitrine
   breast of lamb/veal poitrine d'agneau/de veau
   chicken breast suprême de poulet
brill barbue
brioche brioche
brisket (of beef) poitrine (de boeuf)
brittle nougatine
broad bean grosse fève; fève des marais
broccoli (chou) brocoli
broth bouillon
brown *[verb]* (faire) brunir; (faire) dorer
brown bread pain complet

brown butter   beurre noisette
brown rice   riz complet
brown sugar   sucre roux, cassonade
brown sauce   sauce espagnole
Brussels sprouts   choux de Bruxelles
bubble and squeak   choux et pommes de terre frits
buckwheat   sarrasin, blé noir
buffet   buffet
bulgar wheat, bulgur wheat   blé concassé
bun   petit pain au lait
burbot   lotte (d'eau douce)
burdock   glouteron, bardane
burgundy (wine)   (vin de) bourgogne; *see also* **wine**
burnet   pimprenelle
burnt   brûlé(e)
butcher's shop   boucherie
butter   beurre
    butter sauce   sauce au beurre
    with butter   avec beurre, au beurre
    without butter   sans beurre
butterfish   blennie
buttermilk   lait de beurre, babeurre

Cc

cabbage   chou
cabinet pudding   pouding cabinet
Caesar salad   salade César
caffeine   caféine
    caffeine-free   sans caféine, décaféiné(e)

cake gâteau
   carrot cake gâteau aux carottes
   cream cake gâteau à la crème
   fruit cake cake *[aux fruits confits]*
   sponge cake génoise
calf veau
   calf's brains cervelle de veau
   calf's liver foie de veau
camomile camomille
canapés canapés
candied confit(e)
   candied peel zeste confit, écorce confite
candle chandelle
candlestick chandelier
candy *[US]* bonbon
cane sugar sucre de canne
canned en boîte (de conserve)
cantaloup (melon) cantaloup
capers câpres
capon chapon
capsicum piment doux, poivron
carafe carafe
caramel caramel
caraway (seeds) cumin des prés, carvi
carbohydrate glucides *[hydrates de carbone]*
cardamom cardamome
carp carpe
carrot carotte
   carrot cake gâteau aux carottes
carve découper
cassata cassate
cashew nut noix d'acajou/noix de cajou
casserole casserole
caster sugar sucre semoule
catfish poisson-chat, silure
catsup *[US]* ketchup, sauce tomate
cauliflower chou-fleur
   cauliflower cheese chou-fleur sauce Mornay, au gratin
caviar caviar
cayenne pepper poivre de cayenne
celeriac céleri-rave

celery céleri
cereal *[breakfast]* céréales
chair chaise
champagne champagne
chantilly (crème) Chantilly
chanterelle chanterelle *[mushroom]*
char *[fish]* omble chevalier
charcoal charbon de bois
   charcoal-grilled grillé(e) au charbon de bois
chard bette, blette
charlotte charlotte
   apple charlotte charlotte aux pommes
cheddar (cheese) (fromage) cheddar
cheese fromage
   cheese board plateau à fromage; plateau de fromages
   cheesecake gâteau au fromage blanc
   cream cheese fromage à la crème
   cheese sauce sauce Mornay
   cheese soufflé soufflé au fromage
   cheese straw paille, allumette au fromage
chef chef
cherry cerise
   cherry brandy cherry brandy, liqueur de cerise
   cherry tomato tomate-cerise
chervil cerfeuil
chestnut *[sweet]* marron, châtaigne
   water chestnut châtaigne d'eau
chickpea pois chiche
chicken poulet
   roast chicken poulet rôti
   breast of chicken suprême de poulet
   chicken gumbo (potage de) poulet et gombo
   chicken Kiev poulet à la Kiev
   chicken livers foies de poulets
   chicken salad salade au poulet
   chicken soup soupe de poulet
chicory endive
children's menu menu des enfants
chilled rafraîchi(e)
chilli piment fort, piment rouge
   chilli con carne chili con carne
   chilli pepper piment fort, piment rouge
   chilli powder piment en poudre

china (service) vaisselle; service de porcelaine
China tea thé de Chine
Chinese cabbage chou de Chine
chipped *[glass, plate]* (verre, assiette) ébréché(e)
chips (pommes) frites
chips *[US]* (pommes) chips
chitterling *[US]* friture de tripes *[découpées en morceaux]*
chives ciboulette, civette
chocolate chocolat
    chocolate eclair éclair au chocolat
    chocolate mousse mousse au chocolat
    chocolate sauce sauce au chocolat
    chocolate truffle truffe au chocolat
chop *[cutlet]* côte, côtelette
chopped (into pieces) en dés; (persil) haché
chopsticks baguettes
choux pastry pâte à choux
chowder soupe de poisson à base de lait
Christmas cake gâteau de Noël *[anglais]*
Christmas log bûche de Noël
Christmas pudding pouding de Noël *[anglais]*
cider cidre
    cider vinegar vinaigre de cidre
cinnamon cannelle
citron cédrat
citrus agrumes
clam clam, palourde
    clam chowder chowder aux palourdes
claret bordeaux rouge
clean propre
clear up desservir (la table)
clear soup consommé
clementine clémentine
clove clou de girofle
    clove of garlic gousse d'ail
cobnut noisette
cockles coques
cocoa (poudre de) cacao
    cocoa butter beurre de cacao
    cup of cocoa une tasse de cacao/de chocolat

coconut noix de coco
  coconut milk lait de coco
  desiccated coconut noix de coco séchée
cod morue, cabillaud
coffee café
  cappuccino coffee cappuccino
  coffee whitener succédané de lait *[en poudre]*
  coffee parfait parfait au café
  coffee pot cafetière
  coffee spoon cuillère à café
  decaffeinated coffee café décaféiné, un déca
  espresso / expresso coffee café express
  filter coffee café filtre
  instant coffee café soluble
cold froid(e)
  cold cuts *[US]* assiette de viandes froides, assiette anglaise
  cold meat viande froide
coley *[coalfish]* lieu noir, colin
collared beef rosbif roulé *[ficelé]*
condensed milk lait condensé
condiment condiment
confectioner's custard crème pâtissière
conger eel congre, anguille de mer
consommé (soup) consommé
  cold consommé consommé froid, consommé en gelée
continental breakfast café complet
cook chef
cookies *[US]* biscuits, gâteaux secs
coriander coriandre
corkscrew tire-bouchon
corn maïs
  corn bread pain à la farine de maïs
  cornflour fécule de maïs
  corn on the cob épi de maïs, maïs en épi
  corn syrup sirop de maïs
corned beef boeuf de conserve
cornet *[ice cream]* cornet (de glace)
cos lettuce (laitue) romaine
cottage cheese fromage 'cottage'
courgette courgette
couscous couscous

83

crab crabe, tourteau, dormeur
  dressed crab crabe froid à l'anglaise/à la russe
  prepared crab crabe décortiqué
crackling couenne croquante (du rôti de porc)
cranberry canneberge
  cranberry sauce sauce de canneberges
crawfish langouste
crayfish écrevisse
cream crème
  double cream crème épaisse
  single cream crème légère
  whipped cream crème Chantilly, crème fouettée
  cream cheese fromage à la crème
  cream cake gâteau à la crème
  cream sauce sauce à la crème *[béchamel]*
  cream slice millefeuille *[où la crème Chantilly remplace la crème pâtissière]*
  cream tea thé accompagné de scones avec confiture et crème fraîche
cream of crème (de), velouté (de)
  cream of asparagus soup crème d'asperges
  cream of chicken soup crème de volaille, velouté de volaille
  cream of tomato soup crème de tomates
creamed en purée, à la crème
  creamed potato *[US]* purée de pommes de terre
  creamed spinach purée d'épinards à la crème
creamy en crème, crémeux(-euse), velouté(e)
crème caramel *[baked custard]* crème caramel
crème fraîche crème fraîche
cress cresson
crispbread biscotte
crisps (pommes) chips
croquette potatoes croquettes de pommes de terre
croutons croûtons
crumble crumble
crumpet petite crêpe épaisse *[non sucrée]*
crystallised fruit fruits confits
cucumber concombre
  cucumber sandwich sandwich au concombre
cumin (seed) cumin
cup tasse
  cup and saucer tasse et soucoupe
  cup of coffee tasse de café; un café

    cup of tea tasse de thé; un thé
    coffee cup tasse à café
    tea cup tasse à thé
cured fumé(e), mariné(e), salé(e)
currants raisins de Corinthe
curry curry, cari
custard crème anglaise
    baked custard flan
    custard apple anone, pomme canelle
    custard sauce crème anglaise
    custard tart tartelette à la crème
cut couper
cutlery couvert
cutlet côtelette
cuttlefish seiche

English-French

Dd

dab limande
dairy products produits laitiers
damson prune de Damas
date datte
date plum kaki
debone désosser, lever les filets
decaffeinated, decaf (café) décaféine, un déca
deep-fried cuit(e) à grande friture
deer chevreuil
defrost dégeler
delicious délicieux (-euse)
demerara sugar sucre roux cristallisé

dessert dessert
   dessert wine vin doux, vin de dessert
devilled (à la) diable
   devilled kidneys rognons à la (sauce) diable
   devilled sauce sauce (à la) diable
diced en cube
dill aneth
   dill sauce sauce à l'aneth
dinner dîner
dip *[verb]* tremper
dip *[noun]* sauce froide *[pour crudités]*
dirty *[adj]* sale
dirty *[verb]* salir
dish plat
   dish of the day plat du jour
dogfish aiguillat, chien de mer
done cuit(e)
   under-done pas assez cuit(e); *[viande]* saignant(e)
   well-done bien cuit(e)
dory, John Dory Saint-Pierre, dorée
double cream crème épaisse
doughnut beignet
   jam doughnut beignet fourré à la confiture
Dover sole sole
draught beer bière (à la) pression
dressing vinaigrette
dried séché(e), sec (sèche)
   sun-dried tomatoes tomates séchées (au soleil)
drink boisson
   drinks included forfait boissons
drumsticks pattes de dinde ou de poulet
dry (wine) (vin) sec
Dublin bay prawn langoustine
duchesse potatoes pommes (de terre) duchesse
duck *[domestic]* canard (domestique)
duck *[wild]* canard sauvage
   duck paté pâté de canard
   duck with oranges canard à l'orange
   duckling caneton, canette *[female]*
dumpling boulette de pâte
   potato dumpling gnocchi Parmentier

Ee

eclair éclair
eel anguille
egg oeuf
    boiled egg oeuf à la coque
    egg and bacon oeuf et bacon
    egg cup coquetier
    egg white blanc d'oeuf
    egg yolk jaune d'oeuf
    fried egg oeuf sur le plat
    hard-boiled egg oeuf dur
    omelette omelette
    poached egg oeuf poché
    scrambled eggs oeufs brouillés
    soft-boiled egg oeuf mollct
eggplant [US] aubergine
elderberry baie de sureau
endive chicorée frisée
entree [starter] entrée
entree [US main course] plat principal
escalope escalope
    turkey escalope escalope de dinde
    veal escalope escalope de veau
essence cxtrait (de)
ewe's milk lait de brebis
    ewe's milk cheese fromage de (lait de) brebis

Ff

faggot ballottine
farm (eggs, chickens) (oeufs, poulets) fermiers
fat *[adj]* gras (grasse)
fat *[noun]* gras
   fat-free sans gras
fennel fenouil
feta cheese (fromage) feta, féta
fig figue
filbert aveline
fillet filet
   fillet steak tournedos, steak prélevé dans le filet
   fillet of beef filet de boeuf
filleted désossé(e), en filets
filo pastry pâte phyllo
filter coffee café filtre
fine beans haricots verts (fins)
fish poisson
   anchovy anchois
   angel fish ange de mer
   bass loup (de mer), bar
   bream brème
   brill barbue
   burbot lotte (d'eau douce)
   catfish poisson-chat, silure
   cod morue, cabillaud
   coley *[coalfish]* colin, lieu noir
   conger eel congre, anguille de mer
   crayfish écrevisse
   cuttlefish seiche

dogfish aiguillat, chien de mer
dory, John Dory Saint-Pierre, dorée
Dover sole sole *[la vraie]*
eel anguille
fish and chips friture de poisson avec frites
fish stew matelote, bouillabaisse
fish soup soupe de poissons
fish cake croquette de poisson
flounder flet
flying fish poisson volant
grey mullet mulet gris
haddock aiglefin, églefin
hake merlu, colin
halibut flétan
herring hareng
kipper hareng saur/fumé
lemon sole limande-sole
mackerel maquereau
monkfish baudroie, lotte de mer
pike brochet
pike-perch sandre
pilchard pilchard, (grosse) sardine
red mullet rouget barbet
rockfish rascasse
roe oeufs de poisson, laitance
salmon saumon
scorpion fish rascasse
sea bass loup (de mer), bar
sea bream brème de mer
sea trout truite de mer, truite saumonée
shark requin, aiguillat
skate raie
skipjack bonite
smelt éperlan
sole sole
sturgeon esturgeon
swordfish espadon
tench tanche
trout truite
tunny, tuna thon
turbot turbot
whitebait *[sprats]* blanchaille
whiting merlan
fisherman's pie timbale de poisson
fish shop poissonerie
fizzy pétillant(e), gazeux(-euse)

English-French

flageolet (beans) flageolet
flakes flocons
flambé flambé(e)
flan flan
flat fish poisson plat
flavour *[of ice cream]* parfum
flavoured aromatisé
floating island(s) oeufs à la neige, île(s) flottante(s)
flounder flet
flour farine
flying fish poisson volant
fondant fondant
fondue fondue
fool mousse faite de fruits, crème anglaise et Chantilly
fork fourchette
fowl volaille
   boiling fowl poule
free-range *(egg, chicken)* (oeuf, poulet) fermier
French beans haricots verts
French dressing vinaigrette
French fries *[US]* (pommes) frites
French toast pain perdu, pain doré
fresh frais (fraîche)
freshwater (fish) (poisson) d'eau douce
fried frit(e)
fried chicken poulet frit
fried egg oeuf sur le plat
fried fish poisson frit
   mixed fried fish friture de poissons
frisée (salad) chicorée frisée
fritter beignet
   apple fritter beignet de pommes
frog's legs cuisses de grenouilles
frozen surgelé(e)
fruit fruit
   fruit cocktail salade de fruits, macédoine de fruits
   fruit juice jus de fruits
   fruit salad salade de fruits, macédoine de fruits
fry frire
fudge fondant au chocolat
full-bodied wine vin corsé

full-cream milk lait entier
full-fat (cheese) (fromage) de lait entier

Gg

galantine galantine
game gibier (à plume, à poil); chevreuil
  game pie pâté de gibier en croûte
gammon jambon fumé (désossé)
garden mint menthe verte
garden peas petits pois frais
garlic ail
garlicky aillé(e)
gateau gâteau
gazpacho gaspacho
gelatine gélatine
ghee beurre clarifié *[cuisine indienne]*
gherkin cornichon
giblets abats
gin genièvre
ginger gingembre
  ginger beer bière au gingembre
  gingerbread pain d'épice(s)
  ginger cake gâteau au gingembre
glacé cherry cerise confite
glass verre
  clean glass verre propre
  glass of water verre d'eau
  wine glass verre à vin
glazed glacé(e)
gluten-free sans gluten

GM *[genetically modified]* génétiquement modifié

goat chèvre
  goat's cheese fromage de chèvre
  goat's milk lait de chèvre

goose oie
  goose liver foie d'oie

gooseberry groseille à maquereau

goulash goulash, goulasch

granary loaf pain complet

granita granité

granulated sugar sucre granulé

grape(s) raisin(s) (de table)

grapefruit pamplemousse

grapeseed oil huile de pépins de raisin

grated râpé(e)

gratuity pourboire

gravy sauce, jus de viande
  gravy boat saucière

Greek yoghurt yaourt à la grecque *[au lait de brebis]*

green beans haricots verts

green olives olives vertes

green peas petits pois

green pepper poivron vert

green salad salade verte

greengage (plum) reine-claude

Greenland halibut flétan noir

greens légumes verts

grenadine grenadine

grey mullet mulet gris

grill *[verb]* griller, cuire sur le gril

grill *[noun]* gril
  mixed grill assiette de viandes grillées (assorties)

grilled grillé(e)

grind moudre

gristle cartilage, croquant

grits *[US]* bouillie de maïs, gruau de maïs

groats gruau d'avoine

grocery épicerie; *[small]* alimentation

ground *[coffee]* moulu(e), *[meat]* haché(e)
  ground beef hachis, boeuf haché

groundnut oil huile d'arachide

grouper mérou
grouse grouse
guava goyave
gudgeon goujon
guinea fowl pintade
gumbo gombo
gurnard grondin

Hh

haddock aiglefin, églefin
haggis haggis *[estomac de mouton contenant un hachis d'abattis de mouton, oignons et avoine, le tout bouilli]*
hake merlu, colin
half bottle demi-bouteille
halibut flétan
ham jambon
   boiled ham jambon poché
   slice of ham tranche de jambon
hamburger hamburger
hard-boiled egg oeuf dur
hard cheese fromage à pâte dure
hard roe oeufs de poisson
hare lièvre
haricot beans haricots blancs
hash browns *[US]* pommes de terre en dés, avec oignons, sautées
haunch cuissot
hazelnut noisette, aveline
heart coeur
heat up chauffer, réchauffer

herbs fines herbes
herbal tea tisane, infusion
herring hareng
hickory nut noix du noyer blanc d'Amérique
hollandaise sauce sauce hollandaise
hominy grits *[US]* bouillie de maïs
honey miel
honeycomb rayon de miel, gaufre de miel
honeydew melon cavaillon
hors d'oeuvre hors d'oeuvre
horse mackerel chinchard
horsemeat viande de cheval, cheval
horseradish raifort
hot *[not cold]* chaud(e); *[strong]* piquant(e)
hot dog hot dog *[saucisse de Francfort dans un petit pain]*
hotpot ragoût (de boeuf), potée

Ii

ice glace
   bucket of ice seau de glace *[pour garder le vin frais]*
ice cream glace, crème glacée
   ice cream cone cornet de glace/de crème glacée
   ice cream scoop boule de glace/de crème glacée
ice cube glaçon
ice lolly Esquimau®
iceberg lettuce laitue iceberg
icing glace, glaçage
   icing sugar sucre glace/en poudre
ingredients ingrédients, éléments

instant coffee   café soluble
Irish stew   ragoût de mouton à l'irlandaise
Irish whiskey   whiskey irlandais

Jj

jam   confiture
jelly *[savoury]*   aspic, chaud-froid, galantine
jelly *[sweet/pudding]*   gelée
jelly *[US, jam]*   confiture
jello *[US]*   gelée *[parfumée à la fraise, etc.]*
Jerusalem artichoke   topinambour
John Dory   Saint-Pierre, dorée
jug   pot
jugged hare   civet de lièvre
juice   jus (de fruits; de viande)
julienne   julienne

Kk

kaki   kaki, plaquemine
kale   chou vert frisé *[non pommé]*
kebab   kébab, brochette (de viande)
kedgeree   riz au poisson fumé avec oeufs durs et cari
ketchup   ketchup
key lime pie   tarte à la crème de citron vert
kidney   rognon
kidney beans   haricots rouges
king prawn   crevette rose
kipper   hareng fumé, hareng saur
kiwi fruit   kiwi
knife   couteau
knuckle   jarret
kohlrabi   chou-rave
kosher   casher, kasher
kumquat   kumquat

LI

lactose lactose
  lactose intolerance intolérance au lactose
ladies fingers gombos
lager bière blonde
  a lager shandy un demi panaché
lamb agneau
  lamb chop côtelette d'agneau
lamb's lettuce mâche
langoustine langoustine
lard saindoux
lark alouette
lasagne lasagne
latte (coffee) café crème
lavatory toilettes, WC, lavabo
lavender lavande
leek poireau
leg patte
  leg of lamb gigot d'agneau
legumes légumineuses
lemon citron
  lemon balm mélisse
  lemon grass citronnelle
  lemon juice jus de citron
  lemon sole limande-sole
  lemon zest zeste, écorce de citron
  lemonade limonade; *[freshly squeezed]* citron pressé
lentil lentille
lettuce laitue, salade

97

lime citron vert, lime
ling lingue
light-bodied wine vin léger
liqueur liqueur
liquorice réglisse
liver foie
   liver sausage leberwurst
loaf pain
   meat loaf pain de viande
   white loaf pain blanc, pain de mie
lobster homard
   lobster bisque bisque de homard
loganberry loganberry
loin (of veal/pork/venison) longe (de veau/porc/chevreuil)
low-fat *[diet]* basses calories; *[yoghurt etc.]* allégé
low in fat qui contient peu de gras; basses calories
low-salt qui contient peu de sel; hyposodé(e)
lunch déjeuner, lunch
luncheon meat viande froide pressée *[de conserve]*
lychee litchi, letchi

Mm

macadamia nuts noix du noyer de Queensland
macaroni macaroni
macaroon macaron
mace macis
mackerel maquereau
macrobiotic macrobiotique

Madeira madère
   Madeira cake génoise au citron, gâteau de Savoie
   Madeira sauce sauce madère
maize maïs
mallard colvert
malt malt
mandarin mandarine
mangetout pois gourmands, pois mange-tout, mangetouts
mango mangue
mangosteen mangouste, mangoustan
maple syrup sirop d'érable
maple sugar sucre d'érable
margarine margarine
marinated mariné(e)
marjoram marjolaine
market marché
marmalade marmelade d'oranges, confiture d'oranges
marrow *[vegetable]* courge
marrow bone os à moelle
   bone marrow moelle
Marsala wine marsala
marshmallow guimauve
marzipan massepain
mashed en purée
mashed potatoes pommes purée
matches allumettes
matchstick potatoes pommes allumettes
mayonnaise mayonnaise
mead hydromel
meal repas
meat viande
   meat ball boulette de viande
   meat loaf terrine/pain de viande
   meat pie tourte/pie de viande
medallion médaillon
medlar nèfle
melon melon
melted butter beurre fondu
menu menu, carte
   set menu menu à prix fixe
meringue meringue

milk lait
   cow's milk lait de vache
   ewe's milk lait de brebis
   goat's milk lait de chèvre
   soya milk lait de soja
   milk chocolate chocolat au lait
   poached in milk poché dans du lait
   with milk avec (du) lait; au lait
   without milk sans lait
minced meat hachis, viande hachée
mincemeat mincemeat *[préparation sucrée à base d'un mélange de fruits et raisins secs, et de suif]*
mince pie mince pie *[tarte(lette) avec mincemeat]*
mineral water eau minérale
   fizzy mineral water eau gazeuse
   still mineral water eau plate
minestrone (soup) (soupe) minestrone
mint menthe
   mint sauce sauce à la menthe (fraîche)
   mint jelly gelée à la menthe
mixed grill assiette de viandes grillées (assorties)
mixed salad salade composée
mixed vegetables macédoine de légumes
mollusc mollusque
monkfish baudroie, lotte de mer
morels morilles
mousse mousse, mousseline
muesli müesli
muffin *[sweet, savoury]* muffin
mug mug, tasse *[sans soucoupe]*
mulberry mûre *[du mûrier]*
mullet rouget
mulligatawny (soup) potage au cari
mushroom champignon
   button mushrooms champignons de Paris
mushy peas purée de pois
mussel moule
mustard moutarde
mutton mouton

Nn

napkin   serviette (de table)
natural   nature
Neapolitan ice cream   tranche napolitaine
neat   sans eau ni glace
nectarine   brugnon, nectarine
nettle   ortie
no smoking   défense de fumer
non-smoking area   section non fumeurs
noodles   nouilles
nut   noix
    almond   amande
    Brazil nut   noix du Brésil
    cashew nut   noix d'acajou, noix de cajou
    chestnut   marron
    cobnut   noisette
    coconut   noix de coco
    hazelnut   noisette, aveline
    peanut   arachide, cacah(o)uète
    pecan nut   noix de pécan, noix de pacane
    sweet chestnut   châtaigne, marron
    walnut   noix
nutmeg   noix de muscade

Oo

oatcake biscuit à la farine d'avoine *[pour manger avec le fromage]*
oatmeal farine d'avoine
oats avoine
  porridge oats flocons d'avoine
octopus poulpe
oil huile
okra gombo
olive olive
  black olives olives noires
  green olives olives vertes
olive oil huile d'olive
omelette omelette
on the rocks *[with ice]* avec glace, on the rocks
onion oignon
  onion soup soupe à l'oignon
orange orange
  orange juice jus d'orange
  orange sauce sauce à l'orange; *[less sweet]* sauce bigarade
oregano origan
organic biologique
ostrich autruche
oven four
overdone trop cuit(e)
oxtail queue de boeuf
  oxtail soup soupe à la queue de boeuf
ox tongue langue de boeuf
oyster huître
oyster mushroom pleurote

Pp

pancake crêpe
pan-fried à la poêle, poêlé(e)
papaya papaye
paprika paprika
par-boiled pré-cuit(e), mi-cuit(e)
parfait parfait
Parma ham jambon de Parme
Parmesan (cheese) parmesan
parsley persil
   curly parsley persil frisé
   flat parsley persil plat
   parsley sauce sauce au persil *[béchamel fortement persillée]*
parsnip panais
partridge perdrix; *[young]* perdreau
pasta pâtes (alimentaires)
   fresh pasta pâtes fraîches
pastry pâtisserie
   filo pastry pâte phyllo
   puff pastry pâte feuilletée
   shortcrust pastry pâte brisée
pasty chausson avec viande et pommes de terre
pâté pâté
   liver pâté pâté de foie gras
pawpaw papaye
pea pois
   green peas petits pois
   green pea soup potage St Germain
   split peas pois cassés
   pea soup *[with split peas]* soupe aux pois (cassés)

103

peach pêche
peanut arachide
   peanut butter beurre de cacahouètes/d'arachides
pear poire
pearl barley orge perlée
pease-pudding purée de pois cassés
pecan nut noix de pécan, noix de pacane
   pecan pie tarte aux noix de pécan
peel *[verb]* peler, éplucher
peel *[noun]* pelure, peau, écorce
   grated peel zeste, écorce râpée
peeled sans pelure, sans peau
pepper *[spice]* poivre
   black/green/white pepper poivre noir/vert/blanc
   ground pepper poivre moulu
   whole pepper poivre en grains
   pepper mill moulin à poivre
   pepper pot poivrière
   pepper steak steak au poivre
pepper *[vegetable]* poivron
   green pepper poivron vert
   red pepper poivron rouge
   stuffed pepper poivron farci
peppermint menthe poivrée
perch perche (d'eau douce)
perry cidre de poire
persimmon plaquemine, kaki
pesto pistou
petits fours petits fours
pheasant faisan
pickled cabbage choucroute
pickled gherkin/cucumber cornichon (saumuré/au vinaigre)
pickled herring hareng mariné
pickled onion oignon au vinaigre
pickles pickles
pie tarte, tourte
pig porc, cochon
   suck(l)ing pig cochon de lait, porcelet
pigeon pigeon
pig's trotters pieds de porc
pike brochet
pike-perch sandre

pilchard pilchard, (grosse) sardine
pineapple ananas
pistachio (nut) pistache
pitcher pichet, carafe
pitta bread pain grec *[sans levain]*
plaice plie, carrelet
plain nature
plantain banane verte *[à cuire]*
plate assiette
plum prune
plum pudding plum pudding, pouding de Noël
plum tomato tomate oblongue, tomate allongée
poach pocher
poached poché(e)
poached egg oeuf poché
polenta polenta, semoule de maïs
pollack lieu
pomegranate grenade
popcorn *(sweet/salted)* maïs soufflé (sucré/salé)
porcini mushroom cèpe
pork porc
   pork chop côte de porc
   pork crackling couenne croquante (du rôti de porc)
porridge porridge, bouillie d'avoine
port (vin de) porto
pot roast viande en cocotte
potato pomme de terre
   baked potato pomme de terre au four
   boiled potatoes pommes de terre à l'anglaise
   fried potatoes pommes de terre sautées
   mashed potatoes purée de pommes de terre, pommes purée
   new potatoes pommes de terre nouvelles
   potato chips (pommes) frites
   potato crisps (pommes) chips
   potato dumpling gnocchi Parmentier
   potato salad salade de pommes de terre
potted shrimp petite terrine de crevettes au beurre
poultry volaille
pound cake gâteau quatre-quarts
poussin poussin
prawn bouquet, crevette rose
   Dublin bay prawn langoustine

preserves conserves
price prix
prime rib côte de boeuf *[première qualité]*
profiteroles profiteroles
prune pruneau (sec)
pudding *[savoury]* pouding
pudding *[sweet]* dessert, pouding, pudding
pudding rice riz rond
pudding wine vin de dessert, vin doux
puff pastry pâte feuilletée
pulses légumineuses
pumpkin potiron, citrouille
purslane pourpier

English-French

Qq

quail caille
   quails' eggs oeufs de cailles
quark quark, fromage blanc
quiche quiche
   quiche lorraine quiche lorraine
quince coing
Quorn® aliment à base de protéines végétales

Rr

rabbit lapin; *[young]* lapereau
rack carré
   rack of lamb carré d'agneau
   rack of ribs carré (d'agneau, de porc)
radicchio trévise, chicorée rouge
radish/radishes radis
ragout ragoût
rainbow trout truite arc-en-ciel
raisin raisin sec
ramekin ramequin
rancid rance
rare *[steak, meat]* saignant(e)
raspberry framboise
ravioli ravioli
raw cru(e)
recipe recette
red cabbage chou rouge
red chilli piment fort, piment rouge
redcurrant groseille rouge
   redcurrant jelly gelée de groseilles
redfish rascasse
red mullet rouget barbet
red pepper poivron rouge, piment doux rouge
red wine vin rouge
reindeer chevreuil
rhubarb rhubarbe

ribs côtes
   rack of ribs carré (d'agneau, de porc)
   ribs of beef côtes de boeuf, entrecôtes
   spare ribs travers de porc, côtes levées
rice riz
   long-grained rice riz Caroline
   rice paper papier de riz
   rice pudding pouding au riz; riz au lait *[cuit au four]*
   risotto rice riz pour risotto *[riz rond du Piémont]*
   wild rice riz sauvage
rind *[cheese]* pâte
ripe mûr(e)
rissole rissole
river rivière; *[fish]* d'eau douce
roast *[verb]* rôtir
roast *[noun]* rôti de boeuf/porc etc
   roast beef rôti de boeuf, rosbif
   roast chicken poulet rôti
   roast pork rôti de porc
roasted rôti(e)
rock salt sel gemme
rocket roquette
rockfish rascasse
roe oeufs de poisson
   hard roe oeufs de poisson
   soft roe laitance
roll *[bread]* petit pain
rolled oats flocons d'avoine
rollmop herring rollmop, hareng roulé (mariné)
romaine (lettuce) romaine
room temperature chambré(e)
rosé (wine) (vin) rosé
rosehip fruit de l'églantier
rosemary romarin
rum rhum
   rum baba baba au rhum
rump steak romsteak
runner bean haricot grimpant
rusk biscotte *[pour bébé]*
rye seigle
rye bread pain de seigle, pumpernickel
rye whisky rye *[whisky de seigle]*

Ss

saccharin saccharine
saddle râble (de lapin); selle (d'agneau)
safflower carthame
saffron safran
sage sauge
sago sagou
saithe lieu noir
salad salade
   green salad salade verte
   mixed salad salade composée, salade panachée
   salad dressing vinaigrette
   salad cream crème mayonnaise
   side salad salade verte *[en accompagnement]*
salami saucisson italien
salmon saumon
   salmon steak darne de saumon
   salmon trout truite de mer, truite saumonée
salsify salsifis
salt sel
   low-salt hyposodé(e)
salted salé(e), avec sel
sand sole sole *[plus petite que la 'vraie sole']*
sandwich sandwich
   cheese sandwich sandwich au fromage
   ham sandwich sandwich au jambon
sardine sardine
sauce sauce
   white sauce (sauce) béchamel, sauce blanche

saucer soucoupe
saury balaou
sausage saucisse
  liver sausage leberwurst
  sausage roll friand
sautéed sauté(e), au sautoir
sauté pan sautoir
saveloy cervelas
savoury entremets salé
savoy cabbage chou vert frisé *[pommé]*
scallion *[US]* ciboule, cive
scallop coquille St Jacques
scalloped chicken *[US]* poulet en sauce blanche, au four
scalloped potatoes *[US]* gratin dauphinois
scampi queues de langoustine, scampi
scone *[UK]* scone *[petit pain qu'on mange avec confiture et crème]*
scorpion fish rascasse
Scotch à l'écossaise
  Scotch broth potage de mouton, légumes et orge
  Scotch egg oeuf en croquette *[oeuf (dur) enrobé de chair à saucisse, pané et frit]*
scrambled eggs oeufs brouillés
sea bass loup (de mer), bar
sea bream brème de mer
seafood fruits de mer
sear (faire) saisir
seasoning assaisonnement
sea trout truite de mer
seaweed algue
semi-skimmed milk lait demi-écrémé
semolina semoule
service service
  service discretionary service à la discrétion du client
  service included service compris
  service not included service non compris
serviette serviette (de table)
sesame seeds graines de sésame
shad alose
shallot échalote
shandy panaché
  a half of shandy un demi panaché

shark requin, aiguillat
sharp fort(e), acide
shellfish crustacé, coquillage, fruits de mer
shepherd's pie hachis Parmentier
sherbet sorbet, granité
sherry xérès
shiitake mushrooms champignons chinois (shiitake)
shop magasin
shortbread sablé
shortcrust (pastry) pâte brisée
shoulder épaule, palette
shrimp crevette (grise)
  shrimp cocktail crevettes mayonnaise
sift tamiser
silverside gîte à la noix
simmer (laisser) mijoter
single cream crème (légère)
sirloin aloyau, faux-filet
skate raie
skewer brochette
skimmed milk lait écrémé
skin peau, pelure
skipjack bonite
slice tranche
  slice of bread tranche de pain
  slice of pie part de tarte
  slice of ham tranche de jambon
sliced tranché(e)
sloe prunelle
  sloe gin eau de vie de prunelle
smelt éperlan
smoked fumé(e)
  smoked bacon lard fumé
  smoked cheese fromage fumé
  smoked eel anguille fumée
  smoked fish poisson fumé
  smoked haddock aiglefin fumé
  smoked kipper hareng saur, hareng fumé
  smoked meat viande fumé
  smoked salmon saumon fumé
snack *[light meal]* repas léger; *[between meals]* casse-croûte
snail escargot

English-French

snipe bécassine
soda bread pain au bicarbonate de soude
soda water eau de seltz
soft-boiled egg oeuf à la coque
soft cheese fromage à pâte molle
soft drink boisson (gazeuse) non alcoolisée
soft roe laitance
sole sole
sorbet sorbet
sorghum sorgho
sorrel oseille
soufflé soufflé
   cheese soufflé soufflé au fromage
soup soupe, potage
   soup spoon cuillère à soupe
   broth bouillon
   chowder soupe de poisson et légumes à base de lait
   consommé consommé
   fish stock court-bouillon
   fish soup soupe de poisson(s)
   mulligatawny potage au cari
   onion soup soupe à l'oignon
   vegetable soup soupe de légumes; minestrone
   vichyssoise vichyssoise
sour aigre
   sour cream crème aigre
   sweet and sour aigre-doux (-douce)
soya bean (fève de) soja
soya milk lait de soja
soya sauce sauce soja
spaghetti spaghetti
spare ribs travers de porc, côtes levées
sparkling pétillant(e)
   sparkling water eau gazeuse
   sparkling wine vin mousseux, vin pétillant
spice épice
spicy épicé(e)
spinach épinard
spiny lobster langouste
sponge biscuits biscuits à la cuillère
sponge cake gâteau mousseline; génoise
spoon cuillère, cuiller

sprat   sprat, harenguet, anchois de Norvège
spring greens   jeunes feuilles de choux, brocolis, etc.
spring onion   ciboule, cive
spring water   eau de source
sprouts (Brussels)   choux de Bruxelles
squab   pigeonneau
squash   courge
squid   calmar, encornet
stale   rassis(e)
starter   entrée
steak *[beef]*   bifteck, steak
steak and kidney pie   pie de bifteck et rognons
steak and kidney pudding   pouding de bifteck et rognons
steamed   (cuit) à la vapeur
stew *[meat]*   fricassée, ragoût
    lamb stew   navarin
stewed   *[meat]* (en) fricassée; *[fruit]* en compote
    stewed fruit   compote de fruits, fruits en compote
    stewed steak   fricassée/ragoût de boeuf
Stilton   fromage stilton
stir-fry   sauter à la chinoise
stock   bouillon
    vegetable stock   bouillon de légumes
stout   stout *[bière brune]*
straight *[US]*   sans eau ni glace
strawberry   fraise
    strawberry jam   confiture de fraises
    strawberry shortcake   gâteau fourré aux fraises, recouvert de
    crème Chantilly
streaky bacon   lard de poitrine, poitrine fumée
strip steak   entrecôte
stuffed   farci(e), fourré(e)
    stuffed olives   olives farcies
stuffing   farce
sturgeon   esturgeon
suck(l)ing pig   cochon de lait, porcelet
suet   suif (de boeuf)
sugar   sucre
    caster sugar   sucre semoule
    granulated sugar   sucre granulé
    icing sugar   sucre en poudre, sucre glace

sugar snap peas   petit pois gourmands, pois mange-tout
sultanas   raisins de Smyrne
sundae   coupe glacée
sunflower   tournesol
   sunflower oil   huile de tournesol
supper   dîner, souper
supplement   supplément
swede   navet (de Suède), rutabaga
sweet   sucré(e), doux (douce)
   sweet (wine)   (vin) doux, vin de dessert
   sweet chesnut   châtaigne, marron
   sweet potato   patate douce
   sweet trolley   desserts *[présentés sur une table roulante]*
sweet and sour   aigre-doux (-douce)
sweetbreads   ris de veau
sweetcorn   maïs (en épis, en grains)
sweetener *[artificial]*   édulcorant
swiss roll   (gâteau) roulé
swordfish   espadon
syllabub   syllabub, sabayon
syrup   sirop

Tt

table   table
   tablecloth   nappe
   tablespoon   cuillère à dessert
   table wine   vin de table
tagliatelle   tagliatelle
tangerine   tangerine
tapioca   tapioca

tarragon estragon

tart tartelette

tartar sauce sauce tartare

tea thé
  afternoon tea (le) thé de 5 heures
  beef tea bouillon de boeuf
  cup of tea tasse de thé
  green tea thé vert
  herbal tea tisane, infusion
  high tea repas de 5 heures *[Ecosse et Nord de l'Angleterre]*
  iced tea thé glacé
  lemon tea thé (au) citron
  teacake brioche *[coupée, grillée, avec beurre, servie avec du thé]*
  teaspoon cuillère à thé
  tea with milk thé au lait
  tea-time heure du thé
  teapot théière

tench tanche

tender tendre

tenderloin filet (de boeuf, de porc)

terrine terrine

thrush grive

thyme thym

tin boîte de conserve

tinned en boîte (de conserve)

tip pourboire

toad in the hole saucisses couvertes de pâte *[au four]*

toast pain grillé
  French toast pain perdu, pain doré

toffee caramel (au beurre)

tofu tofu, pâté de soja

tomato tomate
  tomato juice jus de tomate
  tomato ketchup ketchup, sauce tomate
  tomato salad salade de tomate
  tomato sauce sauce (à la) tomate

tongue langue *[de boeuf]*

toothpick cure-dent(s)

tope milandre

tough *[meat]* dur(e)

treacle mélasse
  treacle tart tarte au sirop de maïs

trifle trifle *[génoise, fruits, Chantilly]*
trimmings accompagnement, garniture
tripe tripes, gras-double
trout truite
truffle truffe
   chocolate truffle *[sweet]* truffe (au chocolat)
   truffle butter beurre de truffes
tuna, tunny thon
turbot turbot
turkey dinde
   roast turkey dinde rôtie
turmeric curcuma
turnip navet
   turnip tops fanes de navet
turnover chausson (aux pommes, etc.)

English-French

Uu

uncooked cru(e); qui n'est pas cuit(e)
underdone pas assez cuit(e)
unsalted butter beurre sans sel
upside-down cake gâteau renversé

Vv

vanilla vanille
   vanilla essence extrait de vanille *[liquide]*
   vanilla ice cream glace à la vanille
   vanilla pod/bean gousse de vanille
   vanilla sugar sucre vanillé
veal veau
   veal escalope escalope de veau
vegan végétalien (-ienne)
vegetable légume
   vegetable soup soupe de légumes; minestrone
vegetarian végétarien (-ienne)
venison venaison, chevreuil
vermicelli vermicelle
very dry *[wine]* très sec
Victoria sponge (cake) génoise
vinaigrette vinaigrette
vinegar vinaigre
vine leaves feuilles de vigne
virgin olive oil huile d'olive vierge
vol au vent vol-au-vent, bouchée feuilletée
   chicken vol au vent bouchée à la reine

Ww

wafer gaufrette
waffles gaufres
waiter garçon, serveur
waitress serveuse
Waldorf salad salade Waldorf (pommes, céleri, noix, avec mayonnaise)
walnut noix; cerneau (de la noix)
warm *[salad etc.]* tiède
water eau
    bottled water eau en bouteille
    fizzy water eau gazeuse
    glass of water verre d'eau
    iced water eau glacée, très froide
    jug of water carafe d'eau
    mineral water eau minérale
    sparkling water eau gazeuse
    spring water eau de source
    still water eau plate, eau non gazeuse
watercress cresson de fontaine
watermelon pastèque
well done bien cuit(e)
Welsh rarebit/rabbit pain avec fromage grillé
whale baleine
wheat blé
whelk buccin
whipped cream crème Chantilly, crème fouettée
whisky whisky écossais
whitebait *[sprats]* blanchaille
white blanc (blanche)
    white bread pain de mie, pain blanc

white meat   viande blanche
white wine   vin blanc
whiting   merlan
whole grain mustard   moutarde de Meaux
wholemeal bread   pain complet
whortleberry   myrtille
wild rice   riz sauvage
wild strawberry   fraise des bois, fraise sauvage
wine   vin
  bottle of wine   bouteille de vin
  glass of wine   verre de vin
  house wine   vin (de la) maison
  local wine   vin local, vin de pays
  red wine   vin rouge
  sparkling wine   vin mousseux, vin pétillant
  sweet/pudding wine   vin doux, vin de dessert
  wine cooler   rafraîchisseur *[à vin]*
  wine list   carte des vins
  wine vinegar *[red, white]*   vinaigre de vin (rouge, blanc)
  wine waiter   sommelier
  white wine   vin blanc
winkle   bigorneau
woodcock   bécasse

English-French

YyZz

yam   igname; *[US]* patate douce
yoghurt   yaourt, yogourt
  plain yoghurt   yaourt nature
Yorkshire pudding   yorkshire pudding *[beignet de pâte frite, salé]*
zabaglione   zabaglione, sabayon
zest   zeste
zucchini *[US]*   courgette

Wines and spirits

by John Doxat

Major French wine regions

Alsace

Producer of attractive, light white wines, mostly medium-dry, widely used as carafe wines in middle-range French restaurants. Alsace wines are not greatly appreciated overseas and thus remain comparatively inexpensive for their quality; they are well placed to compete with popular German varieties. Alsace wines are designated by grape – principally Sylvaner for lightest styles, the widespread and reliable Riesling for a large part of the total, and Gewürtztraminer for slightly fruitier wines.

Bordeaux

Divided into a score of districts, and sub-divided into very many *communes* (parishes). The big district names are Médoc, St Emilion, Pomerol, Graves and Sauternes. Prices for the great reds (châteaux Pétrus, Mouton-Rothschild, etc.) or the finest sweet whites (especially the miraculous Yquem) have become stratospheric. Yet 'château' in itself means little and the classification of various rankings of châteaux is not easily understood. Some tiny vineyards are entitled to be called château, which has led to disputes about what have been dubbed 'phantom châteaux'. Visitors are advised, unless wine-wise, to stick to the simpler designations.

Bourgogne (Burgundy)

Topographically a large region, stretching from Chablis (on the east end of the Loire), noted for its steely dry whites, to Lyons. It is particularly associated with fairly powerful red wines and very dry whites, which tend to acidity except for the costlier styles. Almost to Bordeaux excesses, the prices for really top Burgundies have gone through the roof. For value, stick to simpler local wines.

Technically Burgundies, but often separately listed, are the Beaujolais wines. The young red Beaujolais (not necessarily the over-publicised *nouveau*) are delicious when mildly chilled. There are several rather neglected Beaujolais wines (Moulin-à-Vent, Morgon, St Amour, for instance) that improve for several years: they represent good value as a rule. The Mâconnais and Chalonnais also produce sound Burgundies (red and white) that are usually priced within reason.

Champagne

So important is Champagne that, alone of French wines, it carries no AC (*appellation contrôlée*): its name is sufficient guarantee. (It shares this distinction with the brandies Cognac and Armagnac.) Vintage Champagnes from the grandes marques – a limited number of 'great brands' – tend to be as expensive in France as in Britain. You can find unknown brands of high quality (often offshoots of grandes marques) at attractive prices, especially in the Champagne country itself. However, you need information to discover these, and there are true Champagnes for the home market that are doux (sweet) or demi-sec (medium sweet) but are pleasing to few non-French tastes. Champagne is very closely controlled as to region, quantities and grape types, and is made only by secondary fermentation in the bottle. Since 1993, it is prohibited (under EU law) to state that other wines are made by the 'champagne method' – even if they are.

Loire

Prolific producer of very reliable, if rarely great, white wines, notably Muscadet, Sancerre, Anjou (its *rosé* is famous), Vouvray (sparkling and semi-sparkling), and Saumur (particularly its 'champagne styles'). Touraine makes excellent whites and also reds of some distinction – Bourgueil and Chinon. It used to be widely believed a rumour put out by rivals? – that Loire wines 'did not travel': nonsense. They are a successful export.

Rhône

Continuation south of Burgundy. The Rhône is particularly associated with very robust reds, notably Châteauneuf-du-Pape, and also with Tavel, arguably the finest of all still rosé wines. Lirac rosé is nearly as good. Hermitage and Gigondas are names to respect for reds, whites and rosés. Rhône has well earned its modern reputation – no longer Burgundy's poorer brother. From the extreme south comes the newly 'smart' dessert *vin doux naturel,* ultrasweet *Muscat des Beaumes-de-Venise,* once despised by British wine-drinkers. There are fashions in wine just like anything else.

Minor regions

Bergerac

Attractive basic reds; also sweet Monbazillac, relished in France but not easily obtained outside: aged examples can be superb.

Cahors

Noted for its powerful *vin de pays* 'black wine', the darkest red made.

Corsica

Roughish wines of more antiquity than breeding, but by all means drink local reds – and try the wine-based aperitif Cap Corse – if visiting this remarkable island.

Gaillac

Little known; once celebrated for dessert wines.

Jura

Virtually unknown outside France. Try local speciality wines such as *vin jaune* if in the region.

Jurançon

Remote area; sound, unimportant white wines, sweet styles being the better.

Midi

Stretches from Marseilles to the Spanish border. Outstandingly prolific contributor to the 'EU wine lake' and producer of some 80 per cent of French *vins de table*, white and red. Sweet whites dominate, and there is major production of *vins doux naturels* (fortified sugary wines).

Paris

Yes, there is a vineyard – in Montmartre! Don't ask for a bottle: the tiny production is sold by auction, for charity, to rich collectors of curiosities.

Provence

Large wine region of immense antiquity. Many and varied *vins de pays* of little distinction. Best known for rosé, usually on the sweet side; all inexpensive and totally drinkable.

Savoy

Good enough table wines for local consumption. Best product of the region is delicious Chambéry vermouth: as an aperitif, do try the well distributed Chambéryzette, a unique vermouth with a hint of wild strawberries.

Spirits

The great French spirit is brandy. Cognac, commercially the leader, must come from the closely controlled region of that name. Of various quality designations, the commonest is VSOP (very special old pale): it will be a cognac worth drinking neat. Remember, *champagne* in a cognac connotation has absolutely no connection with the wine. It is a topographical term, with *grande champagne* being the most prestigious cognac area; *fine champagne* is a blend of brandy from the two top cognac sub-divisions. Armagnac has become better known lately outside France, and rightly so. As a brandy it has a much longer history than cognac: some connoisseurs rate old armagnac (the quality designations are roughly similar) above cognac.

Be cautious of French brandy without a cognac or armagnac title, regardless of how many meaningless 'stars' the label carries or even the magic word 'Napoleon' (which has no legal significance).

Little appreciated in Britain is the splendid 'apple brandy', Calvados, mainly associated with Normandy but also made in Brittany and the Marne. The best is *Calvados du Pays d'Auge*. Do taste well-aged Calvados, but avoid any suspiciously cheap.

Contrary to popular belief, true Calvados is not distilled from cider – but an inferior imitation is. French cider (cidre) is excellent.

Though most French proprietary aperitifs, like Dubonnet, are fairly low in alcohol, the extremely popular Pernod/Ricard pastis-style brands are highly spirituous. Eau-de-vie is the generic term for all spirits, but colloquially tends to refer to local, often rough, distillates. Exceptions are the better *alcools blancs* (white spirits), which are made from fresh fruits and not sweetened as *crèmes* are.

Wine

Glossary of French wine terms

Abricotine
Generic apricot liqueur: look for known brands.

alcool blanc
Spirit distilled from various fruits (not wine) such as plums and raspberries; not fruit-flavoured cordials.

Aligoté
Light dry Burgundy.

Alsace
See **Major French wine regions**, p122.

anis
Aniseed, much favoured in pastis (Ricard/Pernod) type aperitifs.

Anjou
See **Loire**, **Major French wine regions**, p123.

aperitif
Literally 'opener': any drink taken as an appetiser.

Appellation (d'origine) Contrôllée
or AC wine, whose label will give you a good deal of information, will usually be costlier – but not necessarily better – than one that is a VDQS 'designated (regional) wine of superior quality'. A newer, marginally lesser category is VQPRD: 'quality wine from a specified district'. Hundreds of wines bear AC descriptions: you require knowledge and/or a wine guide to find your way around. The intention of the AC laws was to protect consumers and ensure wine was not falsely labelled – and also to prevent over-production. Only wines of reasonable standards should achieve AC status: new ones (some rather suspect) are being regularly admitted to the list.

Armagnac
See **Spirits**, p125.

Barsac
Very sweet Sauternes of varying quality.

Basserau
A bit of an oddity: sparkling red Burgundy.

Beaumes-de-Venise
Well-known vin doux naturel; *see* **Provence**, **Minor regions**, p124.

Beaune

Famed red Burgundy; costly.

Bergerac

Sound red wine from south-west France.

Blanc de Blancs

White wine from white grapes alone. Sometimes confers extra quality but by no means always. White wine made from black grapes (the skins removed before fermentation) is Blanc de Noirs. Carries no special quality connotation in itself.

Bordeaux

See **Major French wine regions**, p122.

bouchonné

Corked (describes wine that has gone 'off' and smells musty, usually because of a faulty cork allowing in bacteria)

Bourgeuil

Reliable red Loire wine.

Bourgogne

Burgundy; *see* **Major French wine regions**, p122.

brut

Very dry; description particularly applicable to best sparkling wines.

brut sauvage

Dry to the point of displeasing acidness to most palates; very rare though a few good wines carry the description.

Cabernet

Noble grape, especially Cabernet-Sauvignon for excellent, if not absolutely top-grade, red wines.

Cacao

Cocoa; basis of a popular crème.

Calvados

See **Spirits**, p125.

cassis

Blackcurrant; notably in crème de cassis (*see* **kir**).

cave

Cellar.

Cépage
Indicates grape variety; e.g. Cépage Cabernet-Sauvignon.

Chablis
See **Burgundy, Major French wine regions**, p122.

chai
Ground-level storehouse, wholly employed in Cognac and sometimes in Bordeaux and other districts.

Champagne
See **Major French wine regions**, p123. Also note **Méthode Traditionnelle** below.

Chardonnay
Popular, now international grape variety producing dry to buttery white wines.

Château(x)
See **Bordeaux, Major French wine regions**, p122.

Châteaneuf-du-Pape
Best known of powerful Rhône red wines.

Chenin-blanc
Grape variety associated with many fine Loire wines.

Clairet
Unimportant Bordeaux wine, its distinction being probable origin of English word *claret*.

clos
Mainly a Burgundian term for a vineyard formerly (rarely now) enclosed by a wall.

Cognac
See **Spirits**, p125.

Corbières
Usually a sound south of France red wine.

côte
Indicates vineyard on a hillside; no quality connotation necessarily.

côteau(x)
Much the same as above.

crème

Many sweet, sometimes sickly, mildly alcoholic cordials with many local specialities. Nearer to true liqueurs are top makes of crème de menthe and crème de Grand Marnier (q.v.). Crème de cassis is mixed with white wine to produce kir, or with a sparkling white wine to produce kir royal.

Crémant

Sparkling wine with strong but rather brief effervescence.

cru

Literally 'growth'. Somewhat complicated and occasionally misleading term: e.g. *grand cru* may be only grower's estimation, *cru classé* just means the wine is officially recognised, but *grand cru classé* is most likely to be something special.

cuve close

Literally 'sealed vat'. Describes production of sparkling wines by bulk as opposed to individual bottle fermentation. Can produce satisfactory wines and certainly much superior to cheap carbonated styles.

cuvée

Should mean unblended wine from single vat, but *cuvée spéciale* may not be particularly special: only taste will tell.

demi-sec

Linguistically misleading, as it does not mean 'half-dry' but 'medium sweet'.

digestif

Liqueur or brandy drunk after a meal to aid digestion.

Domaine

Broadly, Burgundian equivalent to Bordeaux château.

doux

Very sweet.

eau-de-vie

Generic term for all distilled spirits but usually only applied in practice to roughish marc (q.v.) and the like.

Entre-deux-Mers

Undistinguished but fairly popular white Bordeaux.

frappé

Drink served with crushed ice; e.g. crème de menthe frappée.

Fleurie

One of several superior Beaujolais wines.

glacé

Drink chilled by immersion of bottle in ice or in refrigerator, as distinct from frappé above.

goût

Taste; also colloquial term in some regions for local eau-de-vie (q.v.).

Grand Marnier

Distinguished orange-flavoured liqueur. *See also* **crème**.

Haut

'High'. It indicates upper part of wine district, not necessarily the best, though Haut-Médoc produces much better wines than other areas.

Hermitage

Several excellent Rhône red wines carry this title.

Izarra

Ancient Armagnac-based liqueur much favoured by its Basque originators.

Juliénas

Notable Beaujolais wine.

kir

Well-chilled dry white wine (should be Bourgogne Aligoté) plus a teaspoon of crème de cassis (q.v.). Made with champagne (or good dry sparkling wine) it is kir royal.

liqueur

From old liqueur de dessert, denoting postprandial digestive. Always very sweet. 'Liqueur' has become misused as indication of superior quality: to speak of 'liqueur cognac' is contradictory – yet some very fine true liqueurs are based on cognac.

Loire

See **Major French wine regions**, p123.

marc

Mostly coarse distillations from wine residue with strong local popularity. A few marcs ('mar') – de Champagne, de Bourgogne especially – have achieved a certain cult status.

marque
Brand or company name.

Méthode Traditionnelle
Since the labelling ban prohibiting the use of the term 'champagne method' for wines made outside the Champagne district, this term is used for superior sparkling wine made in the same way as champagne, by fermentation in bottle.

Meursault
Splendid white Burgundy for those who can afford it.

Minervoise
Respectable southern red wine: can be good value as are many such.

mise
As in *mise en bouteilles au château* ('château-bottled'), or ... *dans nos caves* ('in our cellars') and variations.

Montrachet
Very fine white Burgundy.

Moulin-à-Vent
One of the rather special Beaujolais wines.

Muscadet
Arguably the most popular light dry Loire white wine.

Muscat
Though used for some dry whites, this grape is mainly associated with succulent dessert-style wines.

Nouveau
New wine, for drinking fresh; particularly associated with now tiring vogue for Beaujolais Nouveau.

pastis
General term for powerful anis/liquorice aperitifs originally evolved to replace banned absinthe and particularly associated with Marseilles area through the great firm of Ricard.

pétillant
Gently, naturally effervescent.

Pineau

Unfermented grape juice lightly fortified with grape spirit; attractive aperitif widely made in France and under-appreciated abroad.

Pouilly-Fuissé

Dry white Burgundy (Macon); sometimes over-valued.

Pouilly-Fumé

Easily confused with above; a very dry fine Loire white.

porto

Port wine: usually lighter in France than the type preferred in Britain and popular, chilled, as an aperitif.

primeur

More or less the same as nouveau, but more often used for fine vintage wine sold en primeur for laying down to mature.

rosé

'Pink wine', best made by allowing temporary contact of juice and black grapes during fermentation; also by mixing red and white wine.

Sauvignon

Notable white grape; *see also* **Cabernet**.

sec

'Dry', but a wine so marked will be sweetish, even very sweet. Extra Sec may actually mean on the dry side.

sirop

Syrup; e.g. sugar-syrup used in mixed drinks, also some flavoured proprietary non-alcoholic cordials.

Supérieur(e)

Much the same as Haut (q.v.) except in VDQS.

VQRPD

See **Appellation (d'origine) Contrôllée** above, p128.

vin de Xeres

Sherry ('vin de 'ereth').

French Cheeses

How can anybody be expected to govern a country that has 246 kinds of cheese?

(Charles de Gaulle)

France is one of the biggest cheese producers in the world. Since de Gaulle's original comment in 1962 the number of types of cheese it offers has grown to around 500.

French cheeses fall into six main categories:

- fresh cream cheeses such as petit-suisse
- surface-ripened soft cheeses such as Brie and Camembert
- washed-rind soft cheeses such as Pont l'Evêque
- goat's cheeses such as Crottin de Chavignol
- blue cheeses such as Roquefort and Bleu d'Auvergne
- cooked and uncooked pressed cheeses such as Comté and Reblochon, with a firm texture.

Fresh cheeses are made from unpasteurised milk and do not undergo any ripening or fermentation process. Surface-ripened cheeses are allowed to ripen for a few weeks until a white mould, called a bloom, forms. Washed-rind cheeses are repeatedly washed in warm salt water to encourage a firm rind to form. Pressed cheeses are pressed in a mould for up to 12 months; in the case of cooked cheeses they are heated before being pressed.

Like the best French wines, the quality of French cheeses is tightly regulated and the top 40 carry the 'Appellation d'origine contrôlée' mark (AOC). This means that their origin and quality is strictly controlled and guarantees, among other things, that the cheese originates from a specific region of France and has been produced using traditional methods.

Cheese

The criteria laid down for AOC cheeses are rigorous:

- The cheese has to come from a geographically precise area such as a municipality or a district. The milk must come from this particular region too and the cheese must be produced and partly matured there as well.

- The production methods have a strong influence on the characteristics of a cheese. In order to ensure top quality, AOC cheeses have to be made by strictly defined methods that have been handed down over centuries.

- The size, type of rind, texture and minimum fat content of the cheese are all responsible for its final flavour. These characteristics are precisely defined and have to be adhered to strictly by producers, who are inspected by Ministry of Agriculture staff responsible for monitoring the authenticity and quality of the products.

The current AOC cheeses are listed here, together with the type of milk used to make them and the area they originate from.

Cheese	Description	Origin
Abondance	hard cow's milk cheese produced from unpasteurised milk, with fruity nutty flavour	Haute Savoie (eastern France)
Beaufort	hard cow's milk cheese produced from unpasteurised milk, with fruity aromatic flavour	Savoie (eastern France)
Bleu d'Auvergne	semi-soft blue cheese from unpasteurised cow's milk, with full nutty flavour	Auvergne (central France)
Bleu de Gex	semi-soft cheese made from unpasteurised cow's milk, with a distinctive hazelnut flavour	Rhône-Alpes/Jura

Cheese

Cheese	Description	Origin
Bleu des Causses	semi-soft blue cow's milk cheese, stronger than Bleu d'Auvergne	Midi-Pyrénées
Bleu du Vercors	semi-soft blue cow's milk cheese with mild nutty flavour	Rhône-Alpes
Brie de Meaux	soft surface-ripened cheese from unpasteurised cow's milk, with mild fruity taste	Ile-de-France
Brie de Melun	like Brie de Meaux but with stronger smell	Ile-de-France
Brocciu	soft cream cheese made from unpasteurised sheep or goat's milk	Corsica
Camembert de Normandie	soft surface-ripened cheese from unpasteurised cow's milk	Normandy
Cantal	firm drum-shaped cheese from unpasteurised cow's milk	Auvergne
Chabichou du Poitou	soft cone-shaped cheese from unpasteurised goat's milk, with mild flavour	Poitou-Charente (west France)
Chaource	soft surface-ripened drum-shaped cow's milk cheese with delicate flavour	Champagne (north-east France)
Chevrotin	semi-soft cheese of unpasteurised goat's milk	Rhône-Alpes
Comté	hard wheel-shaped cheese from unpasteurised cow's milk	Franche Comté
Crottin de Chavignol	soft goat's milk cheese in small cylinder shape, with acidic flavour	central France

Cheese

Cheese	Description	Origin
Epoisses de Bourgogne	soft washed-rind cow's milk cheese with strong smell and rich, mildly alcoholic taste; sold boxed as it becomes runny as it ripens	Burgundy
Fourme d'Ambert	semi-soft blue cow's milk cheese, cylindrical, with tangy flavour	Auvergne
Fourme de Montbrison	semi-soft blue cow's milk cheese, cylindrical, milder than Fourme d'Ambert	Auvergne
Laguiole	semi-soft drum-shaped cheese made from unpasteurised cow's milk, with tangy flavour	southern Auvergne
Langres	soft washed-rind cow's milk cheese that is sunken on top, a strong smell and a tangy flavour	Champagne/ Burgundy region
Livarot	soft cylindrical cow's milk cheese with washed rind and a pungent smell; ripens to a strong, spicy flavour; bound with leaves	Pays d'Auge (Normandy)
Maroilles	square soft cow's milk cheese with washed rind and a strong flavour	northern France
Mont d'Or	soft unpasteurised cow's milk cheese with a buttery flavour, sold boxed; becomes runny as it ripens	Rhône-Alpes

Cheese

Cheese	Description	Origin
Morbier	firm cheese from unpasteurised cow's milk, with distinctive dark stripe through the middle and a mild fruity flavour	Franche-Comté
Munster	soft unpasteurised cow's milk cheese with washed, strong-smelling rind; often eaten with caraway seeds	Alsace-Lorraine
Neufchâtel	semi-soft surface-ripened heart-shaped cow's milk cheese with slightly tangy taste	Normandy
Ossau-Iraty	round firm sheep's milk cheese with nutty flavour	Pyrénées
Pélardon	soft unpasteurised goat's milk cheese, often eaten baked	Languedoc-Roussillon
Picodon	soft disc-shaped goat's milk cheese with fresh acidic flavour, often grilled	Rhône-Alpes
Pouligny Saint-Pierre	soft cone-shaped goat's milk cheese with nutty flavour	central France
Pont l'Evêque	square soft cow's milk cheese with a washed rind that has a pungent aroma, and a mild flavour	Normandy
Reblochon	semi-soft cheese from unpasteurised cow's milk with creamy, fruity taste	Savoie
Rocadamour	soft cheese made from unpasteurised goat's milk with nutty, acidic taste	Midi-Pyrénées

Cheese

Cheese	Description	Origin
Roquefort	semi-soft blue sheep's milk cheese with strong salty flavour	Midi-Pyrénées
Saint-Nectaire	semi-soft cow's milk cheese with mild flavour	Auvergne
Saint-Maure de Touraine	log-shaped soft unpasteurised goat's milk cheese with grey rind and straw in centre	Touraine (central France)
Salers	firm cheese from unpasteurised cow's milk, similar to Cantal	Auvergne
Selles-sur-Cher	small round soft goat's milk cheese	Loire
Vacherin du haut Doubs	same as Mont d'Or	
Valençay	pyramid-shaped soft goat's milk cheese with ash-covered rind and a mild nutty flavour	central France

Apart from the top 40 listed above, here are some other well-known French cheeses you are likely to encounter:

Cheese	Description	Origin
Cantadou	cow's milk cheese in small balls that can be used as a spread	non-regional
Caprice des Dieux	oval mild soft white cheese	Champagne-Ardennes
Chaumes	full-flavoured soft cow's milk cheese with washed rind and buttery flavour	Périgord
Coulommiers	a smaller Brie-type cheese	Ile-de-France
Etorki	firm sheep's milk cheese	French Basque region

Cheese

Cheese	Description	Origin
Le Pié d'Angloys	soft full-fat cow's milk cheese that ripens in its box	Burgundy
Mimolette	Edam-type cow's milk cheese, dark orange when mature	north-east France (originally Lille)
Port Salut	mild semi-soft cow's milk cheese	non-regional
Raclette	firm cow's milk cheese, often used in cooking as it melts easily	Auvergne
Saint Agur	semi-soft blue cow's milk cheese with mild creamy flavour	Auvergne
Saint Felicien	soft unpasteurised cow's milk cheese with fresh flavour	Burgundy
Saint Marcellin	soft round cow's milk cheese	Dauphine
Saint-Paulin	mild semi-soft cow's milk cheese	mainly Brittany and Normandy
Tomme (de Savoie)	firm unpasteurised cow's milk cheese with hard grey rind and creamy taste	Rhône-Alpes
Vignotte	semi-soft cow's milk cheese with a rich creamy flavour	Champagne

V French cheeses for vegetarians

The French AOC mark generally implies that a cheese has been made with animal rennet, so vegetarians have to search further afield for cheeses that are suitable to eat. Look for commercial brands such as Boursin, Tartare and Saint-Morêt. Companies such as Milleret (who make le Gylois, le Charcennay, le Roucoulous and l'Ortolan), Rippoz (who make Emmenthal, Morbier, Raclette and Tendre), OMA, Guilloteau and Entremont all produce cheeses made with non-animal-based rennet.

Serving cheese

The French eat their cheese before, or in place of, the dessert course.
Cheese can be eaten with bread, or sometimes just on its own, and
should be served at room temperature.

Different cheeses go with different types of bread: for example a soft
creamy cheese such as Neufchâtel or Chaource goes well with fruit or
nut bread. Cheese connoisseurs in particular like to eat the rind, so do
not remove it before serving. Some rinds however are more suitable
for eating than others.

Ideally a cheese should be divided up so that each piece has some
rind on it.

- Small round cheeses such as Camembert or some goat's
  cheeses can be cut into portions from the centre like cakes

- Square cheeses such as Pont l'Evêque can also be cut
  diagonally, then each half sliced into smaller triangles

- Cheeses with a soft rind that have been cut from a larger
  'wheel', such as Brie, are sliced starting from the narrowest
  point of the triangle

- Blue cheeses such as Roquefort are also cut into triangles,
  fanning out from the centre of the narrower end

- Firmer cheeses such as Comté are cut across in straight
  slices, with the thickest slice then cut into two so that each
  piece shares some rind

- Log-shaped cheeses – mainly goat's cheeses such as
  Sainte-Maure – are sliced across into rounds. The smaller,
  round, goat's cheeses should simply be cut into halves or
  thirds

- Divide pyramid- or cone-shaped cheeses such as Pouligny
  Saint-Pierre into vertical triangles starting from the middle,
  so they do not crumble

- Cheeses sold in boxes, such as Epoisses and Mont d'Or, can
  be eaten straight from the box with a spoon if they are
  sufficiently ripe.

Cheese

Serving wine with cheese

As a general rule of thumb it is safe to assume that a cheese will go well with local wines from the same region. Another general guideline is that the stronger the cheese, the more full-bodied the wine should be to balance it. Heavy sweet white wines such as Sauternes go surprisingly well with a range of cheeses, including strong blue cheeses.

Soft surface-ripened cheeses such as Brie go well with light or medium-bodied reds such as Beaujolais or Médoc. Another good principle is to match washed-rind cheeses or firm cheeses such as Munster, Reblochon and Tomme with full-bodied reds such as Saint-Emilion or Châteauneuf-du-Pape, or with white Alsace wines.

Goat's cheeses can be accompanied by Sauvigon blanc or Chardonnay wines, or other dry and fruity white wines. Blue cheeses can either be partnered with a full-bodied red or – a famously successful combination – with a sweet white wine such as Sauternes.

Cheese